"Covers all aspects of cat life, from the initial acquisition through the traumas of life. It is, however, far more than a survival kit for cats and their owners. . . . A pleasure and a joy to read."

The Chattanooga Times

"In readable, informal style that mixes research findings with on-the-job experience, she offers advice about understanding the domestic feline, overcoming its worst traits and appreciating everything about it. . . . Pleasant and informative reading."

The Baltimore News American

"Ms. Randolph misses nothing. Starting with early training, routine grooming and teaching a cat how to show affection from kittenhood on, author Randolph details all aspects of daily care."

Cat's Magazine

"The appeal of Randolph's work lies in its sections on the psychological aspects of living with a cat, and the different problems of indoor and outdoor pets."

Library Journal

HOW TO BE YOUR CAT'S BEST FRIEND

Elizabeth Randolph

FAWCETT CREST · NEW YORK

Drawings by Colleen M. Ahern.
Lines from "For a Yellow Cat at Midnight" by Jean Burden originally appeared in *Southern Review*, May, 1971, and are reprinted by permission of the poet; "Portrait of a Young Cat" by Elizabeth Coatsworth is from *Night and the Cat*, 1950, reprinted by permission of Elizabeth Coatsworth Beston; "A Domestic Cat" by Edwin Denby is from *An Anthology of New York Poets*, edited by Ron Padgett and David Shapiro, 1970; reprinted by permission of Random House, Inc.; "The Rum Tum Tugger" and "Macavity: The Mystery Cat" by T. S. Eliot are from *Old Possum's Book of Practical Cats*, copyright 1939 by T. S. Eliot, renewed 1967 by Esme Valerie Eliot, reprinted by permission of Harcourt Brace Jovanovich. Inc., "On a Cat Ageing" by Alexander Gray is reprinted by permission of John Gray; *"Last Words to a Dumb Friend"* by Thomas Hardy is from *Complete Poems of Thomas Hardy*, edited by James Gibson, 1978, reprinted by permission of Macmillan Publishing Co., Inc.; "The Whole Duty of Kittens" by Oliver Herford is from *The Kitten's Garden of Verses*, copyright 1911 by Oliver Herford, renewal copyright 1939 by Beatrice Herford Hayword, reprinted by permission of Charles Scribner's Sons; "The Happy Cat" by Randall Jarrell is from *The Complete Poems of Randall Jarrell*, copyright © 1969 by Mrs. Randal Jarrell, reprinted by permission of Farrar, Straus and Giroux, Inc.; "In Honour of Taffy Topaz" by Christopher Morely is from *Songs for a Little House*, 1917, 1945, published by J. B. Lippincott Co., reprinted by permission of Harper & Row Publishers, Inc.; "The Kitten" by Ogden Nash, from *Verses From 1929 On*, copyright 1940 by the Curtis Publishing Co., first appeared in *The Saturday Evening Post*, reprinted by permission of Little, Brown and Company; "Cat's Dream" by Pablo Neruda is from *Pablo Neruda; A New Decade (Poems 1958–1967)*, 1969, reprinted by permission of Grove Press, Inc., "Waiting for It" by May Swenson is from *New and Selected Things Taking Place*, copyright © 1958 by May Swenson, reprinted by permission of Little, Brown, and Company, in association with the Atlantic Monthly Press; "Indoor Jungle Blues" by Ulrich Troubetzkoy originally appeared in the *United Church Herald*, 1970, and is reprinted by permission of the poet.

Library of Congress Catalog Card Number: 80-39490

ISBN 0-449-21824-4

Manufactured in the United States of America

First Ballantine Books Edition: February 1990
Fourth Printing: June 1991

To Wilbur,
the "expert" from whom I learned the most about loving
cats

CONTENTS

SECTION II Caring for Your Cat's Physique

Psychological Problems • Problems with the Facilities •
Retraining a Cat Who's Broken Training

SECTION III   Coping with Some Other Aspects of Cat Care

ACKNOWLEDGMENTS

I'd like to thank the following people:

For enthusiastic picture-taking, Elizabeth Jacobson.

For encouragement and editorial advice, Renée V. Overholser.

And most especially, for constant support and help, my husband, Arthur M. Hettich.

INTRODUCTION

The smallest feline is a masterpiece.
—LEONARDO DA VINCI
from his *Notebooks*

Cats can be extremely satisfactory, loving, and congenial pets when they're brought up to be. But they need help from their owners in order to develop into truly responsive companions. If you're a serious cat owner, you'll want to establish a mutually agreeable relationship with your pet. To do this, you should know something about her needs, both physical and emotional. In turn, you'll have to be able to communicate your requirements and expectations to her. This book is for the cat owner who wants to go beyond the usual, everyday physical care of a pet. It will enable you to become your cat's "best friend," and, of course, to help your cat to become yours.

The primary responsibility for establishing a good relationship with your cat rests on you. You're the one who'll set the tone, and it will help a great deal if you can make intelligent decisions about your cat's care and upbringing that are based on her real needs. Cats' "childhoods" are extremely short, and it's during this

1

brief period that they learn just what to expect from the world around them. Their long memories can be both a help and a hindrance to you in raising your pet—good early associations will stay with your cat throughout her lifetime, but so will bad ones.

In writing this book, I've drawn on my long experience as a writer about pets and as a cat owner. In addition, I've included many of the newest findings about feline nutrition and health. This book deals with more than just specifics about health and diet, however; it also has suggestions throughout on how to cope with behavioral problems, such as "bad" behavior and jealousy.

There are some aspects of cat ownership that are not included. There's nothing about feline genetics, breeding of cats, showing of cats, or breeds of cats except where a particular breed characteristic is significant in some way.

I feel very strongly that breeding should be left to professionals. No more "casual" cat breeders are needed—there's already a tragic overpopulation of unwanted cats in this country. The most important favor you can do for yourself and your pet is to have her or him neutered at the appropriate age.

Even though there are some differences in temperament and care requirements for various pedigreed cats, all cats need basically the same diet and health care, and they all respond well to affectionate, thoughtful handling. It's best to learn about any specific needs your pedigreed cat may have from her breeder.

There are many good books in print (see Appendix) about the natural history of cats, breeding and showing, individual breeds, and complete medical care. This book is none of these. It's simply a book about developing a good friendship with your pet.

Introduction

If you're a brand-new cat owner, or a potential one, you may find it helpful to read through the entire book at once. If you're an old hand, you'll probably want to check only the topics of special interest to you and your pet. Whichever kind of reader you are, I think that you'll find that this book contains just about everything you need to know about sensible, satisfying cat ownership.

Step one in the process is choosing your pet wisely.

Choosing a Cat

> The trouble with a kitten is
> THAT
> Eventually it becomes a
> CAT.
> —OGDEN NASH

The fact that all kittens are appealing and cute can be a problem. Unfortunately, many cat owners are stuck with an unsatisfactory cat because they were taken in by a cute kitten. It pays to remember that an average cat today can live for as long as twenty years, so when you take home that cute kitten, you'll be selecting a feline companion who'll be sharing your life for a long time. If you think about that, you'll be more careful not to bring home the first appealing kitten you see.

Unfortunately, casually bred kittens often don't turn into very satisfactory adult pets. When a kitten is born in a restaurant parking lot, the back room of a butcher shop, or even someone's home, to a badly nourished young mother cat who's had three litters in rapid succession, she's off to a very bad start. Not only will poor nutrition probably affect her life expectancy and general health, but her mother's understandable lack

3

of interest will generally mean that the kitten has never been given essential early training in personal care and hygiene. Sad to say, you'll probably find yourself with a kitten who hasn't the slightest idea what a litter tray, or even the outdoors, is for; more important, your new kitten is apt to develop serious health and personality problems. A kitten who hasn't learned from her mother to trust humans may never be able to respond to your love and attention in an affectionate way.

Even those of us who should know better can be charmed into making mistakes. I made a mistake when I chose Francis, our current "second" cat. I first saw him in the veterinarian's office when I took our little dog in for a booster shot. An adorable, tiny, light gray kitten bounced out from behind the reception desk, danced around and hissed at the dog, then rolled over and started to purr. It seems that he'd been left on the doctor's doorstep several days before, and was waiting to find a home. One of our cats had just died, and we'd talked about getting another, so I thought, "Wonderful. This kitten will fit right into our multianimal household and won't be intimidated." He was very cute, seemed to be a toughie—well able to cope despite his size—so I took him home.

What I neglected to find out was if he was used to people. It turned out that he wasn't at all afraid of the other animals, to whom he soon became devoted. The only trouble was that he didn't much like people. He hated being picked up, would barely tolerate being petted, and never sought human companionship. Three years later, he's finally hand-tamed and doesn't cringe when you try to pet him. Occasionally now he'll even seek a human out for attention. This isn't a real problem for us, because Wilbur, our other cat, more than makes up for Francis's lack of feline companionship and affection. But if Francis were an only pet, we'd be sorely disillusioned about the joys of cat ownership.

It pays to consider several things before you go out to select a cat. First, you'll want to decide if you want a breed or a plain cat. Plain cats, by the way, can now be pedigreed, and are called "domestic short-hairs." If you decide that you want any kind of pedigreed cat, you should realize that there's something more than color or length of coat to choose from. Generations of controlled breeding have resulted in some generally accepted overall temperament and personality traits common to each kind of cat, and by selecting a kitten of a particular breed, you can have some idea of what kind of adult cat you'll end up with. If you decided that you want a pedigreed cat, be very careful to go to a breeder with a good reputation who is registered with one of the many cat clubs and/or associations in the United States. Good cat breeding requires knowledge and care. Careless breeding can result in poor specimens: injudicious inbreeding, for instance, can produce sickly kittens.

There are upwards of thirty different cat breeds,* each of which has certain temperamental as well as physical characteristics. There are breeds that are non-allergenic, such as the Rex and Tonkinese. There are long-hairs whose fur doesn't mat, which makes grooming a less arduous daily task, like Birman or Balinese cats. There are noisy, demanding cats who need a lot of attention and entertainment—most Siamese and Rexes fill this category; and there are calm, quiet, undemanding cats, like many long-hairs and Russian Blues. Of course, like any generalizations,

*Because there's no central national registering agency for cats (like the AKC for dogs), the various associations and their member clubs set the standards and groupings for their own shows. Therefore, there's no set number of universally accepted breeds.

these personality traits don't always hold true—I've known quiet, shy Siamese and extroverted, clowny long-hairs.

To find out more about individual breeds, go to a cat show and talk to breeders and owners. Even better, see if you can't visit owners of the breed you're interested in to watch how the cat fits into a household situation. The purchase of a pedigreed cat can represent quite a sizable investment, so it pays to choose carefully.

Since you're undoubtedly going to have your pet neutered, the sex of your kitten won't make much difference. Altered males make delightful, sweet pets; so do spayed females. Most important, whether you choose pedigreed or plain, male or female, is the kitten's own personality and temperament.

You can tell a great deal about a kitten by watching her with other cats. Try to see a kitten with her mother and littermates. Don't pick the smallest and shyest of the litter because you feel sorry for her. A very shy cat is apt to be easily scared and hard to train—everything you say will frighten her. On the other hand, the bully of the litter may be too aggressive to make a good pet unless you're willing to be very tough. A lively, playful kitten who can hold her own with her littermates is usually the best choice. The mother should be a people-cat; kittens learn attitudes from their mother's responses. Don't be tempted to take your new pet home too soon—it's important for kittens to stay with their mother until they're at least seven to eight weeks old, when they're completely weaned.

If you can't arrange to see a kitten with her mother and siblings, you can still learn a lot about her by careful observation and handling. Pick her up. If she struggles to get free and seems frightened, she's probably not used to being handled; if she purrs and clings to you, you'll know that she's already accustomed to people. Put her on the ground. Does she scuttle low and run for cover, or does she act interested in her surroundings and unafraid? One of our sons takes credit for picking Wilbur out of about twenty kittens in a cage at the pound. Some of the others were cuter, but Wilbur won our hearts by rubbing against the side of the cage, purring wildly when we approached, and clinging and rubbing his face against us when we picked him up.

Once you've decided that you like a particular kitten, look her over carefully for signs of ill health. A healthy kitten is clean-looking with bright eyes, firm mouth, shiny coat and smooth skin, no runny nose, clear ears that are shiny on the inside, a solid but not bloated tummy, and straight, firm-feeling legs and spine. Don't assume that scabs or bare patches on skin or coat, or a sniffly nose, will go away with your good care. A kitten who seems sick may be suffering from a number of things, all of which can be difficult and costly to cure. Some things, such as a heart murmur, can be detected only by a veterinarian with a stethoscope. That's why it's important to take your new pet straight to the doctor on your way home. It can be very sad to become attached to a kitten (and it doesn't take long), only to discover that she's seriously ill. Spare yourself and your family that heartache by checking a kitten's health before taking her home.

If you want a companionable, responsive, healthy kitten to raise and live with, take your time to choose carefully. Then your own gentle handling and reinforcement can continue to turn your cat into a real people-cat who'll charm and delight you for the rest of her life.

SECTION ONE

Caring for Your Cat's Psyche

With a cat you stand on much the same footing that you stand with a fine and dignified friend; if you forfeit his respect and confidence the relationship suffers.

—CARL VAN VECHTEN,
A Tiger in the House

1

The Importance of Early Conditioning

A good-natured kitten may be worried
into becoming a bad-natured cat.
—CARL VAN VECHTEN,
A Tiger in the House

Experts agree that cats, like many other domestic animals, have various important "socialization" periods. While it's important for a kitten to associate with other cats (mother and littermates) during the early stages of development, it's equally important for good human contact to start young. If a kitten grows up devoid of lots of gentle handing by humans, she'll develop into an aloof and unresponsive cat. On the other hand, a kitten who is petted and played with by a variety of caring humans will invariably end up a real people-cat, trusting, affectionate, and responsive to all humans. This kind of early social conditioning applies in all of its possible forms: if cats grow up with kind dogs, they end up unafraid of most dogs; cats who grow up with the exclusive attention of one person become "one-man" cats, and so forth. Cats certainly form strong attachments to other pets and to people. It may be anthropomorphizing too much to say that they "love" these individuals, but they obviously do care about them and will display affection, concern,

11

and even longing when the object of their attachment is away.

Among the many cats I've known, Grace and Wilbur clearly demonstrate two effects of early conditioning. Grace came to live in our household when she was only six weeks old because her mother died. Up till then, she'd lived with a loving family. About a week after she arrived, there was a serious illness in our family. The consequence was that she was left alone in the house for most of the day with two grown cats and a small dog. Her needs were taken care of, but she received no more than perfunctory attention from the tired humans when they came home. By the time the household returned to normal, Grace was three months old and had become devoted to the pets in the household, by whom she'd actually been raised. Although she eventually did learn to tolerate handling by humans, she was basically scared of and aggressive with most people for the rest of her life. But she was responsive and affectionate with the other pets, allowing the older cats to lick and groom her, and even letting the little dog chew on her ears.

Wilbur, on the other hand, came from a cage in the pound one Christmastime, a pet for one of our sons to take back to college with him. From the age of eight weeks until he was almost grown, Wilbur lived in a school dormitory, being handled, fussed over, talked to, and carried around by scores of young people. When he came home for the summer, he was terrified of the other pets in the house, but couldn't get enough human attention. He soon learned to hold his own with the animals, although Grace bossed him around until she died, but he had never lost his intense devotion to people. At nine, he's still aggressively affectionate, and can talk even the most confirmed cat hater into a grudging pat.

Heredity can, of course, be a factor in a kitten's degree of responsiveness to "affection-conditioning." Some breeds, such as Siamese, almost always demand a great deal of affection and love, while others tend to be more aloof by nature. Offspring of generations of outdoor cats may have a hard time adjusting to life in a household. However, unless there's something congenitally wrong with a kitten (and, just like people, there are some cats who are born "crazy"; I don't think that it's ever been scientifically proved, but I've known two cats quite well who I'm sure were truly insane), learning to respond to humans is a form of conditioning.

Shared Affection

The time and effort you spend getting to know your cat's needs and desires and helping her to learn what you expect and want from her will pay off in a lifetime of shared affection and enjoyment. It's the key to your entire relationship.

This learning process should begin the minute your cat comes to live with you. The first step is to reach a mutual understanding about overt demonstrations of affection. Your pet will take her cues from you, not only because you're bigger, stronger, and control the rations, but also because she wants to please you. Just as any pet does, a cat learns what you want through patient, repeated demonstration, reward, and frequent vocal reinforcement. At the same time, you'll be learning about your pet's particular personality, her likes, dislikes, and moods.

LEARNING TO PLAY GENTLY

With patient teaching, even the most boisterous kitten can learn to play gently with you. When you play together, you should set the tone. Although you may see a group of kittens tumbling vigorously around, biting and pouncing on each other, this is just mock fighting and isn't as rough as it looks. Cats like gentle handling, and humans shouldn't encourage violent play. Tossing a kitten in the air or tumbling her roughly about won't "toughen her up." An owner who regularly plays fiercely with his cat will accomplish one of two things: he'll turn his pet either into a fierce cat who races wildly around and fights back with tooth and claw; or into a timid, withdrawn, hand-shy "scaredy" cat, who shuns and fears human handling. In either case, it should be no surprise if a roughly treated kitten or cat reacts to an extended hand with a bite or scratch.

Velvet Paws

> How do you know that I am a diplomat?
> By the skillful way you hide your claws.
> —EDMOND ROSTAND, *L'Aiglon*, ACT IV

There's no doubt that claws can be a big problem when you play with a cat or kitten. They can even become a nuisance when your pet is resting comfortably on your lap or on top of your feet in bed. A cat's instinctive "kneading" with her paws and claws is likely to be a very painful experience for you.

Kittens, of course, don't know that they can hurt you with their claws, and they are not being "bad" if they accidentally scratch you when playing. Spanking, slapping, or yelling at a kitten who has just drawn your blood with needle-sharp claws will serve no purpose

14

at all, except to confuse the kitten and perhaps make you feel better.

If you're going to play "chase the pencil" or "catch the string" with your young cat, the first thing to do is to put on a pair of gloves to prevent accidental scratching. Then, as your pet leaps on the quarry, claws extended, catch her front feet gently. Stroke and knead the pads very softly until her claws retract, at the same time repeating "velvet paws" (or whatever you like, the words don't matter) over and over again. By repeatedly showing your pet that you don't want claws extended when she's playing with you, she'll eventually learn to respond to the words alone.

The same technique works when your cat happily begins to purr and knead you to shreds. Again, hold her front paws and massage gently until the claws retract, reinforcing your actions with the words you choose. It may take awhile for your pet to react to the words alone, and you'll probably need to repeat the paw massage frequently, but by the time your pet is full-grown, she should understand that you don't like claws in your person, and a simple word will serve as an effective reminder when needed.

Biting

Kittens also have needle-sharp teeth, which may cause problems while playing. Your kitten may bite you accidentally—a case of getting your hand instead of the toy—or she may nip you purposely. Older cats sometimes bite, too, apparently for various reasons. Sometimes a grown cat seems to bite as an affectionate gesture, after being petted or groomed; at other times attention-getting appears to be the cause. It's not unusual for a cat to put her mouth around your finger or

15

hand and bite it very gently, exerting no pressure. Clearly, this is love.

Some cats react very strongly to being touched in certain parts of their bodies and will bite, hard, in response. Grace used to lie in a typical cat position on her back, with her soft white underside exposed, seemingly asking to have it rubbed. Before we could warn them, visitors sometimes leaned down to pat her tummy. Instantly, she'd curl her body, grabbing the poor person's hand in her paws and sinking her teeth into his wrist. The top of a cat's back, just at the base of the tail, is another sensitive area. Maybe some cats are very ticklish, or perhaps it's a sexual response, but whatever the reason, it seems to me that cats with these touchy spots deserve not to be petted there. There's no reason to rub your cat's stomach if she hates it. You should learn to avoid the danger spots and to warn strangers about them.

If a kitten bites you accidentally in play, she's probably not even aware of it, and there's no need to make a big issue out of it. You may not even mind an affectionate nip from an older cat now and then. But when a kitten or cat starts to bite frequently, you'll have to show her that you don't like it. To do this, every time your cat bites, catch her head firmly on either side of the jaw with one hand, and gently tap the tip of her nose with a finger, saying *"No!"* sternly. Cats' noses are very sensitive, so don't overdo it the first few times, but if your pet continues to bite, you'll have to be firmer and tap her nose more than once each time.

A kitten may still bite occasionally out of youthful spirits or forgetfulness, but if a cat continues to bite a lot it's time to take a good, hard look at how you're handling her. Most cats bite seriously only out of fear or pain, as a last resort. Perhaps you're handling your pet too roughly and either frightening or hurting her.

Caring for Your Cat's Psyche

If a cat feels cornered or helpless, she may think that she has to defend herself by biting. Another possibility is that your cat has some undiagnosed illness or injury and is in pain. A persistent biter should be thoroughly examined by a veterinarian to see if there's a physical cause.

"Crazy Fits"—Wild Behavior

Almost every kitten or young cat has at least one or two "crazy fits" (as opposed to convulsions, p. 177) at one time or another. The most common time for these antics is in the evening. She'll tear around the room, along the backs of chairs, over tabletops and up the curtains, sometimes galloping sideways, stiff-legged, all puffed up, with back arched and tail swishing. The results can be very comical, but if you've never seen this kind of behavior before, it can also be a little frightening. The best course of action is simply to let the wildness run its natural course, and the cat will eventually tire herself out and go to sleep.

If you're concerned for your pet's safety, or for your household, and want her to stop, there are several things that may work. A shout or other sharp noise such as a hand-clap or the bang of a spoon against a metal pot may startle a cat into stopping, but it may have just the opposite effect and incite her to wilder actions. One cat I know stopped in her tracks when the lights were turned out, and another needed some water sprinkled on him. Once you have your cat's attention, tell her firmly and quietly to stop, and she usually will.

When the wild behavior happens too often, you should again look at the way your cat is being handled. Too much rough treatment and frantic play can lead to overstimulation and a sort of hysterical reaction. Al-

17

though kittens love to play, it shouldn't be overdone. Let your kitten set the limits on playtime, and respect her desire to stop. Continual loud noises and hectic household activity can fray even the toughest cat's nervous system. She needs to have a place to get away from it all whenever she wants to, and all family members should be taught to respect her need for quiet.

"Crazy fits" can also be brought on by catnip; some cats seem to react badly to this herb, if they eat too much, with very bizarre antics. Usually cats who get "high" on catnip will also experience a severe "down," or depression, later on. Until you know your own pet's tolerance, go easy on the loose catnip.

If your cat's occasional wild behavior is simply due to high kitten spirits, adulthood will generally calm her down. While some of the more highly strung breeds may never outgrow a spree now and then, calm, thoughtful treatment and plenty of attention will do a great deal to prevent even the most energetic cat from having excessive "crazy fits."

LOVING GESTURES

At the same time that you and your cat are reaching an understanding about gentle play, you'll both be learning how to show affection in different ways. Cats are basically sensuous creatures who love to be touched and to touch. A cat, however, won't beg an uninterested human for this kind of attention. If a pat on the head or a slap on the rump is all that you give your cat in the way of demonstrative affection, she'll learn to settle for that. But if this is as far as you're willing to go, you'll never have the pleasure of having your cat unexpectedly come up and kiss you on the nose, or tap your face gently with a soft paw. A cat won't fawn for love, but if you give it to her, she'll return it in constantly surprising and enchanting ways.

The first move will probably be yours. If you have a young kitten whose principal companions up to now have been her littermates, you'll have to start slowly. Older, ungentled cats will need to be handled even more carefully. There's something about being held very tightly that can throw even the calmest cat into a frenzy, so don't try to restrain your cat in order to pet her.

Stroking and Scratching

> At a touch, he explodes like a snapdragon
> into loud purrs.
> —ELIZABETH J. COATSWORTH,
> "Portrait of a Young Cat"

All cats love to be stroked and scratched. While some will sit still for a long time to be petted, others can stay quiet only for a few minutes of handling at a time, and then will shake themselves and walk off for a wash. Sometimes, for no particular reason that you can fathom, a cat won't want to be petted at all. You'll soon learn to recognize your own pet's preferences, and you'll go a long way toward establishing a close relationship if you respect them.

The time to start this mutual discovery is when your pet is relaxed and calm. She can be sitting on your lap or lying near you. Since most animals are accustomed to being touched on the top of the head, start there. Stroke your cat gently on the top of her head, from front to back, pausing to scratch with your fingertips behind each ear, and up and down the top of her nose. You can cup one, or both, hands and stroke over the ears, too, if your cat enjoys this—she may not like having her ears folded down, so don't insist. Many cats also like to have their muzzles and whiskers stroked from front to back. Under the chin comes next. By now, your pet will probably have her neck extended with her chin tilted up. Stroke and scratch her throat all the way down to the space between her front legs.

The top of a cat's body is the most commonly petted area, so now you should move on to that. Long, smooth strokes from head to tail on the back and sides are a good beginning; using two hands to stroke both sides of her body at once will usually please your cat. You can then try scratching her spine with the tips of your fingers, but go easy when you reach the base of the tail. As I said before, this is a particularly sensitive spot for almost all cats. Most seem to like being scratched there and will arch their backs and purr loudly, but an occasional cat will react very negatively. So don't get carried away until you know your pet's preference, or you may be bitten or scratched!

Now move on to your pet's front legs and paws. Your cat may not want to have her legs or feet touched, which isn't unusual. During these initial stroking sessions, skip any area that seems to make your cat restless or uncomfortable: as your pet gets older or gentler or both, she may learn to like being touched in these spots, but don't force. Some cats really enjoy having their front feet massaged. Wilbur, for instance, will often lift a front paw up into my hand to have it rubbed. He likes me to separate each pad and rub between each toe, then massage the entire bottom and top of his foot in a sort of kneading motion. From there, I often rub up and down each front leg, but it's the foot massage that he particularly enjoys.

If your cat is a real sensualist, by now she'll have rolled over onto her back, legs sticking up in the air, inviting a tummy rub. Unless you know for sure that she'll tolerate being touched on the stomach, start off by simply placing your hand, palm down, gently between her front legs. Move your hand slowly back toward the genital area, resting it lightly on her stomach, just in front of her hind legs. If this produces no violent reaction, you can probably assume that your pet likes to be rubbed on her tummy. You can then rub up and down the length of her underside, pausing to pet under each front "armpit," and ending with a circular rubbing motion in the soft tummy area. Always use a very light touch on your cat's underside, never slap or pat hard, and don't use any pressure if you scratch with your fingertips. This is a very sensitive, vulnerable area, and your pet is showing great trust to let you touch it at all.

While your cat is upside down, you can try softly massaging her thighs and back legs. Most cats aren't crazy about having their back legs fooled with, so if yours retracts her legs and acts uncomfortable, stop. Although your pet will eventually have to learn to tolerate being groomed in sensitive areas, you don't want her first petting sessions to be unpleasant. The same is true of the hind feet. You may be able to massage them just as you did the front paws, but you're apt to find that your cat doesn't appreciate it much.

Last but not least is the tail, which many cats enjoy having stroked. Grasp your cat's tail gently in your curled hand and run your fingers down its length, from the base to the tip. The bottom side of cats' tails is another very sensitive spot, so don't apply any pressure there.

Once you've established a regular stroking routine, don't be surprised if your cat wants you to follow exactly the same pattern each time, presenting her paws and rolling over onto her back so that every part of her can be petted in turn. It's a good idea to separate this part of your handling from grooming, by the way, since it can be very frustrating to try to brush your cat's back if she's continually trying to roll over.

Of course, you can't always do a head-to-toe rub-down—neither you nor your cat may have time. In the beginning, however, this kind of closeness can do a great deal to cement your relationship with your pet; to calm down an overexcited kitten or a nervous cat; and to help you learn more about your cat and her particular likes and dislikes.

Using Your Voice

> The cat's asleep; I whisper "kitten"
> Till he stirs a little and begins to purr—
> —RANDALL JARRELL, "The Happy Cat"

Just as you show displeasure with your voice, you can also use it to show affection. The tone of your voice is more important than the actual words, but your cat will soon grow to understand what you mean when you call her "good" or "beautiful." Many people who have well-loved pets talk to them all the time, and, although the animals don't understand the words, they do seem to know that they're being given special attention. Cats will often purr when you speak to them kindly, and it's not at all unusual for them to answer with a muted word or two. Particularly vocal cats frequently greet human and animal friends with a string of chirruppy sounds.

By talking to your cat softly when you're petting her, she'll soon become accustomed to how you sound when you're pleased with her. After that, a few kind words will often serve to satisfy her, even when there's no time for petting.

Make a point of saying your cat's name when you want her to come to you to be petted, even if it's not needed, and repeat her name often. It will help her learn to respond to it. The more your cat associates pleasant things with her name, the sooner she'll learn to come when called.

Affectionate Gestures from Your Cat to You

> Just your foot upon my head
> Softly bids it understand.
> —ALGERNON CHARLES SWINBURNE,
> "To a Cat"

As time goes on, you'll find that you're not the only one who can demonstrate affection. If you haven't been paying enough attention to your cat one day, you may feel her butting you with the top of her head. She may butt your legs if she's on the floor, or she may get up and butt your arm or hand to make you pat her.

If this doesn't work she may then take her paw, claws sheathed, and literally pull at your hand or arm. At this point, no matter how busy you are, you'd better take time out for a petting, or she'll never leave you alone.

Rubbing against you is a more subtle attention-getting device used by most cats. This is not the dangerous habit of twining around your legs, which I'll talk about later on, but is just the gentle rubbing of the side of her head, from muzzle to the ends of her whiskers, against you. She may do this against your legs, hand, or face if you'll let her. This is the highest form of feline flattery. I've read that the cat is marking you as belonging to her by leaving a scent from glands located on her forehead, lips, and chin. In any case, a cat's whiskers are very important sensory organs, and by rubbing them against you, she is getting a closer "feel" of you.

Another way of getting to know you better and showing you how much she cares for you is by licking.

23

Many people think that it's not usual for a cat to lick, but if you've ever observed two friendly cats together, you've probably noticed that they often lick each other affectionately. A loving swipe with a rough, dry cat's tongue can be a really nice experience.

Cats, of course, don't really "kiss," but when your pet gets up on her hind legs in your lap and touches your nose or mouth with hers, it certainly seems as if that's what she's doing! There's no mistaking the affectionate intent when your cat suddenly "kisses" you, and the only acceptable response is a kiss and hug in return.

Some cats will also "hug" you. Wilbur, for instance, stands on his hind legs on the counter, chair back, or my lap, and reaches his front legs up and around my neck, purring and rubbing his face against mine at the same time. If I respond by picking him up, he'll stay for a moment or two, and then want to get down. "Hugging" seems to be a spontaneous gesture of affection, and most cats don't want to prolong it.

Loving cats also like to be physically close to their owners for part of every day. Even "loners" will often sleep at their owners' feet on top of the bedcovers, or sit nearby on a sofa. Often it seems as if a very affectionate cat can't get too close to you. This can sometimes become irritating, if you're trying to sleep or work, for instance, but it can also be comforting and companionable. The trick is to learn how to let your cat know that her nearness is not acceptable at the moment, without hurting her feelings. A gentle shove, accompanied by a "Good girl, not now," will probably work most of the time. Sometimes, however, when your cat is sitting on top of the newspaper you're trying to read, purring loudly, and inching closer and closer to you, you just have to be firm, put her down,

24

and hope that she'll forget your rudeness the next time you're alone and want a warm companion by your side.

Helping Your Cat Learn to Conform

Another important understanding that you'll want to start reaching with your cat right away is in the area of do's and don'ts. Far from being unkind to your pet, teaching her what's expected will help to keep her free from potential harm, and will also avoid the constant tension of her being yelled at for reasons that she doesn't understand. It's really another important way of showing affection.

While most cats need very little discipline, there are some universal feline behavior traits, one or more of which you may want or need to deal with: clawing, chewing, jumping up on things, stealing food, and the dangerous twining around human legs.

Your own particular life-style and your cat's basic temperament will determine just how much training you'll do. Remember that kittens are generally much more high-spirited than older cats, and that boredom can be the beginning of many bad habits in young cats. Providing plenty of attention and playtime can prevent their onset.

At this point it's only fair to note that there are some cats who are extremely hard to train and/or discipline. Usually these hard-headed felines are very active, stubborn, and willful. Highly bred cats most often seem to fall into this category, but I've known many domestic short-hairs who do, too. It doesn't mean that these cats *can't* be trained, but it takes a very strong-willed, single-minded owner to do it. Seemingly oblivious to shouts, scoldings, and even swats, independent cats will either go right on doing whatever it

25

is they want without so much as a pause, or they'll stop briefly, look straight at you as if to say "Don't bother me!" and continue. Faced with this kind of training job, you can do one of two things: grit your teeth and determine to let your pet know who's master, which can take a lot out of both of you; or see to it that your cat is protected from harm and destructive mischief when you're not around, by closing her up in a safe place.

Many cat owners opt to do just that even when they have a pliable pet, rather than try to train their cat not to do certain things. Closing your cat in, or out of, certain rooms can do a great deal to ease the training and learning burden on both of you, at least until your pet is grown and has become more responsive.

BREAKING BAD HABITS

Basically, breaking your cat's bad habits, or preventing unacceptable behavior from becoming a bad habit, consists of three steps: first, stopping her from doing whatever it is you don't want her to do *immediately*, every single time she does it; second, showing her repeatedly what you do want her to do; third, praising her lavishly when she conforms. Consistency is extremely important, and family members should agree on discipline areas and methods. Cats vary a great deal in their response to discipline. Some are so sensitive that one sharp *"No!"* is all that's ever needed. Others need repeated, much harsher, reminders.

Since almost all cats dislike sharp noises, the best way to stop a cat from doing something is to startle her. When you catch your pet doing something forbidden, a firm *"No!"* accompanied by a hand-clap may stop her short. If this produces no results, you'll have to resort to one or more stronger measures. Shooting a stream of water from a water pistol or plastic spray bottle, slapping a rolled-up newspaper sharply on the floor, or tossing a lightweight paperback book or magazine at the offender should work. If you're near enough, a light slap on your cat's rump or a tap on the end of the nose (the method most often used by mother cats) will serve to stop her and to emphasize your *"No!"* Whatever method you use, the aim is to get your cat to stop what she's doing right away, and to associate her action with something shocking and unpleasant.

If your cat's been so startled that she runs off and hides, don't chase her or drag her out of her hiding place, as this will only serve to frighten and confuse her. Wait if necessary, but try to find an opportunity to show her just what it is you *do* want her to do (use the scratching post, for example), instead of the forbidden thing.

It may help you to be more patient if you can remember that your cat isn't being purposely "bad," but is probably exhibiting a perfectly natural feline characteristic. One day, your weeks of patient training will pay off. Your pet will suddenly use the scratching post, bypass the sofa, or ignore the chicken on the kitchen counter. That's the time to let her know just how pleased you are with her by praising and petting her exaggeratedly. To be sure, she may begin to lapse once in a while, but at this point a simple *"No!"* or sometimes just a harsh look will usually be all the reminder that she'll need.

Clawing

> . . . they all insist on, periodically, getting their claws firmly fixed into something and pulling at it furiously.
> —FRANCES AND RICHARD LOCKRIDGE,
> *Cats and People*

Clawing household furnishings can be the most frustrating, hard-to-break cat habit because it's such a basic, instinctive behavior trait. What we call "scratching," "sharpening claws," or "plucking" is actually a combination of several things: exercising and stretching, and at the same time loosening and pulling off bits of claw. It may also serve another purpose: in *The Cat*, Muriel Beadle points out that wild cats mark off their territory by scratching trees and posts while standing upright. This may explain the penchant of house cats to scratch high up on furniture or curtains. The fact that declawed cats still continue to go through the motions of "sharpening their claws" further shows how instinctive this behavior is.

So, although there are a few house cats who don't scratch a great deal, and some indoor-outdoor cats who confine their scratching to the trees, it's pretty safe to assume that your pet is not one of these unusual animals. If your cat's a scratcher, you'll never train her not to scratch at all, but you can teach her where it's acceptable to scratch. Start early, because cats usually adopt one favorite scratching place, and stick to it.

Almost all cats can be taught to use a *scratching post*. Start with a sturdy scratching device (it doesn't have to be a post, but I'll call it that). "Sturdy" is a key word, because once a post has fallen over onto a cat, she'll never go near it again. It must be solid and strong enough to bear the cat's entire grown body weight, plus the extra stress of her pulling motions. Nailing the post down to the floor or attaching it to a wall will make it more secure. Some owners prefer to use a horizontal, rather than vertical, scratching device. While a few cats may get used to this arrangement, it seems to me that an upright post conforms more closely to the way cats usually scratch.

There are good scratching posts on the market, or you can make your own from lumber and a covering. If you opt to make your own, be very sure that the covering is firmly attached, with no nails or fasteners that could come loose. You can use a log with the bark still on, but bits of bark may come off, and the whole thing can be very messy unless you have an out-of-the-way place to put it. Coverings can vary, from carpeting to burlap to cork, but they must be something durable into which the cat can get her claws. An argument against using carpeting as a scratching-post cover is that the cat won't be able to distinguish between that carpet and other carpet which is not to be scratched. I don't think that this is valid, however, because it's the post, not the carpeting, to which the cat is trained. Whatever covering you choose, it should be replaced at the first sign of wear, before it loses its appeal.

Catnip sprinkled on the outside of the post, or placed under the covering if you make your own, will make it more attractive to your cat. A dangling toy, piece of yarn, or spring toy firmly attached to the top of the post will often encourage kittens and cats to start using it.

Because cats almost always scratch when they first wake up, start your training by housing your cat and the scratching post together in a room where there is no other fabric to scratch. Usually the kitchen is best, since it's not completely isolated. Keep your cat in this room when you're not at home or are not prepared to "police" her actions.

At first, your pet won't have the foggiest notion what this strange object is, so she'll have to be shown. Take your cat's front paws, place them on the post, and make scratching motions with them. Dangle something by the side of the post so that, as your pet plays, she can get the feel of the covering with her claws extended. Praise her warmly if she starts to scratch the post. Repeat this process frequently until your cat starts to go to the post and scratch by herself. Continue to praise her lavishly each time you see her using the post.

Once your cat is using the scratching post regularly, you can start to let her out into the rest of the house, under close supervision. If she so much as lays a scratching paw on anything except the post, go into your *"No!"* routine, grab her, carry her to the post, and put her paws on it. Much praise, again, if she then proceeds to use the post.

This can go on for weeks, or months, depending on your individual cat, how much scratching she normally does, how ingrained her bad habits are, and how vigilant you can manage to be. If you have a large house, you may find it a good idea to have more than one post. A highly spirited, very active "clawy" cat may never learn completely, and may need frequent reminders. Some owners find that they can never trust their cats not to scratch when they're unsupervised, and it's easier to confine the cat during their absence.

What about older cats who are already scratchers? A cat who is given the run of a house from the start will probably never learn to use a scratching post exclusively. It's just too easy for a cat left on her own in the house to take a swipe at the couch when you're not around, and before you know it that couch will become "hers." Once a cat has adopted a piece of furniture as her scratching place, it's very difficult to break the habit. For some cats, evading notice may have become quite a game. These "secret scratchers" will seize any opportunity to claw in an unnoticed spot. One day, you'll move the furniture and find the chair back in shreds! In more-than-one-cat households it's hard to be sure who the culprit was. If this becomes a serious problem, you'll have to isolate the cats and retrain them, one at a time.

Unless you decide to forget the whole thing and live with it, as many cat owners do, the first thing is to try to protect your furniture from more damage. Red pepper, mothballs, or other smelly substances may do some good, but often don't. Turning yourself into a twenty-four-hour guard, yelling, clapping, squirting, and throwing things, may be effective but hardly feasible, nor is recovering everything in rawhide. The best stopgap device is to use lightweight plastic covers or plastic spray—cats hate plastic. Carefully trimming your cat's front claws regularly (see Chapter 2) can greatly reduce the damage, but sometimes this causes cats to redouble their scratching efforts. If you're desperate, you may feel that you have to consider a declawing operation (see p. 124).

Best of all, you can train, or retrain, your cat to use a scratching device. It's difficult but not impossible. I know people who've managed to teach their cats to use a scratching post after years of battling for possession of the sofa. You'll have to be indifferent to your older cat's protests, and hardhearted when she won't speak to you for weeks, but retraining can usually be done by following the steps above. It's well worth a serious try if you care about both your furniture and your cat.

Chewing

Many cats aren't chewers, but there are some who persist in trying to chew everything in sight. Until you know whether your pet is a chewer, you'll have to keep a careful eye on her. Aside from causing damage to your possessions, chewing can be a very dangerous activity for a cat. Electric wires and poisonous house-plants can be very tempting.

The best rule to follow about both is to forbid your pet even to get near them. When a cat bats a leaf or electric cord playfully with her paw it may seem harmless, but the next move is often a nip. A "paws off" policy is the safest and surest method of protecting your cat from harm.

Using the same method that you did to stop your cat from scratching, make your pet aware, immediately, that chewing is unacceptable behavior. There are cat trainers who advocate smearing wires and leaves with a smelly or bad-tasting repellent to keep a curious cat away. I think that this is taking a big chance, however, especially when there are potentially fatal results if your pet chooses to ignore the repellent. It's fine for your bedroom slippers, for instance, but not for an electric wire.

You really can't be too careful or firm about this. Until you're sure that your cat won't chew, even when you're not around, there are two things that you can do. You can kitten-proof your entire house, by unplugging or removing any dangling wires and removing dangerous houseplants or putting them completely out of reach. Or, you can close your cat in a wire-free, plant-free room when you're not prepared to supervise her.

Many kittens will chew a lot while they're teething (second teeth come in at about six months). Give a teething kitten something hard to chew on, such as a large dog biscuit or a rawhide toy (be sure that it's nothing that will splinter), and make it clear to her that when she wants to chew, that's what she should chew on.

Substituting something else to play with will often divert a kitten from playing with forbidden objects. As

I said before, boredom and high spirits will often cause kittens to get into trouble.

While most cats will outgrow the chewing urge, some never seem to. I've known grown cats who had an object, such as a sweater or knotted sock, which they chewed on before going to sleep. If your cat is an habitual chewer, be sure to provide her with something safe to chew on that she can call her own.

Jumping

Cats' ability to jump is truly amazing. They can jump seemingly effortlessly straight up, and land delicately and lightly on all four feet. It's a beautiful action to watch, as long as the jumper hasn't landed on top of the refrigerator where you put a roast to keep it safe.

The fact that jumping is an inherent cat talent doesn't mean that you have to tolerate having your cat literally jump anywhere she pleases. But, although keeping your cat off counters or furniture isn't hard to do when you're around, when you're not there it's hard to control her natural instinct to get off the ground to sleep or explore.

An acquaintance who had never had a cat decided recently that it would be nice to have a pet in her apartment to come home to after work. After much debate and discussion, she decided that a cat would be the ideal pet for her, and she bought a kitten. Two weeks later, she called to tell me that it hadn't worked out, and that she'd had to get rid of her pet, because "It kept getting up on things; I even found footprints on the kitchen counter!"

I don't know this person well enough, but I wanted to ask what she expected when she left a kitten alone in an apartment for nine or more hours a day. And, how in the world did she expect an eight-week-old

33

kitten to know where she was supposed to go with nobody around to tell her?

In my opinion, if you don't like cats "up on things," you shouldn't have a cat. Cats jump. They not only jump, but they like to sleep in high, off-the-floor places. In addition, they always explore every nook and cranny of any new place they're in, at least once, and they always "check out" any new object that comes into their home. It may be curiosity, or perhaps it's a holdover from the days spent in the wild, when everything had to be examined to be sure that it was safe to have around.

Whatever the reason, cats invariably jump up on a new chair or sofa before you've even had a chance to test the cushions. Teaching a pet cat not to jump up on a particular piece of furniture can be done, but only by continual monitoring when she's in the room with the object. Each time she starts to jump up, give a sharp *"No!"* and perhaps a hand-clap. If she persists, and makes it up on the furniture, immediately snatch her off and put her on the floor, accompanied by more *"No!'s."* Other harsher methods, described before, may be necessary if your pet continues to try to get up. Never let your cat get up on the furniture in your absence, or your job will become that much harder. If you really want to train a cat to keep off anything, shut her out of the room when you're not around. An easier solution, which some cat owners adopt, is to put a lightweight plastic cover on the furniture when they're not home. Cats will usually avoid anything covered with it. If they don't, at least the upholstery's protected.

Shelves and windowsills housing bric-a-brac or other breakables can be problem areas. Although many adult cats have an uncanny ability to jump up on a shelf of ornaments and sit wedged between two objects without so much as disturbing the dust around them, most

34

young cats and some klutzy older animals don't have this skill. If you have a valuable or well-loved collection of breakable things, it's a good idea to put it in a safe place until you know that you can trust your pet. It's too late to shout *"No!"* as a priceless object comes tumbling down on your frightened cat's head.

In our house, cats have always had to eat their own meals on a section of the kitchen counter so that the dogs wouldn't get at their food. Once a human starts to prepare food, and the counter has been washed off, they know that they're not welcome. If they forget, a word is all that's needed. Since our cats often sleep on our beds and are healthy and clean, I've never worried particularly about germs from them contaminating our food.

Many people don't share this attitude, and want to train their cats to stay completely away from areas where human food is kept and prepared. If you don't want your cat to jump up on kitchen counters at all, don't leave her closed in the kitchen alone. If the kitchen is your pet's room when you're not around, the counters become part of her territory, to be explored and sat upon. You can't expect a cat to live in the kitchen and know that you don't want her to get up on the counters.

If you want to train your cat not to jump on things when you're not around, there are many methods I've heard advocated. They vary considerably, from booby traps, such as mousetraps placed under newspapers or inflated balloons, to more conventional repellents like red pepper or mothballs. In my experience, a determined cat will simply avoid the booby traps or ignore the repellents, but there's no harm in trying if you really want to. As in other areas, if you're not around to reinforce your wishes, training methods don't seem to mean much to a cat. Again, a door separating your cat from the area you don't want her in is the single most effective training tool there is.

Stealing Food

> Honest as a cat when the cream is out of reach.
> —ANON.

> When Human Folk at Table Eat,
> A Kitten must not mew for meat,
> Or Jump to grab it from the Dish,
> (Unless it happens to be fish).
> —OLIVER HERFORD,
> "The Whole Duty of Kittens"

Even if you don't mind your cat's being on the kitchen counters when you're not preparing food, you certainly can't tolerate a thief.

While most cats will behave most of the time while you're around, I've known several otherwise well-trained cats who go completely out of control at the merest whiff of turkey or lamb or fish. They forget everything they've ever known, including their own innate dignity, and make clowns out of themselves scrambling and leaping in order to dive rudely into their favorite food. Some will even reach out a paw and try to snatch a tidbit while you're looking right at them.

Randolph, a Rex cat I know, acts that way about all human food, from potato chips to onion dip. He seems to think that he's perpetually starving to death. (Many Rex cats have insatiable appetites.) It's pretty hard to train this kind of an addict not to steal food. The most sensible solution is banishment until the object of desire is safely stowed in the refrigerator.

Even a well-behaved cat may drive you crazy with loud meows and frantic rubbings when well-loved food is around. Scolding a cat whose mind is filled with visions of drumsticks will fall on deaf ears. Again, removing the cat is by far the most sensible solution.

Until you're absolutely certain that your cat is voice-trained sufficiently *not* to steal food, don't tempt her needlessly.

Jumping out at People's Legs

This is a kitten trait that I find intolerable, probably because when I was about six, I was terrified by a wild kitten named Snoopy who would lie in wait under my bed, then jump out and climb up my pajama legs with needle-sharp claws as I started to get up in the morning. After he tore my mother's stockings for the fifth time leaping at her ankles, he was returned to the store owner who'd given him to us.

I can never understand why some people don't nip this unpleasant habit in the bud immediately, but seem to find it funny and cute. To be sure, most kittens outgrow it, but in the meantime, it's a real trial for anyone coming into their house.

To break a kitten of this habit, grab her every time she runs out at you, hold her firmly, and tap her sharply on the end of the nose, saying *"No!"* very sternly. If you can't grab hold of her, a swat on the rump, accompanied by *"No!"* will do. Don't let her get away with this kind of attack on anyone's ankles, and don't allow other family members to ignore it. If you're really firm, as you will be if it annoys you as much as it does me, you'll be able to cure your kitten after a few scoldings.

Twining around Human Legs

This is more than an annoying habit: it can be dangerous. Cats who twine around your legs when you're going downstairs or are walking across the kitchen carrying a heavy pan filled with hot grease can cause severe damage not only to you, but to themselves as well. I've known several people who've had nasty falls, and one who even suffered a displaced retina falling over a cat. I've also known cats who've been scalded or had bones broken by getting underfoot.

Cats usually twine because they want attention, but owners are often loath to discipline them because they interpret twining as a gesture of affection. Whatever the reason, some cats tend to get underfoot more than others, and sooner or later someone's going to get hurt.

I've found the most effective method for breaking cats of this dangerous habit is to insert your foot under the cat's belly as soon as she starts to twine, and literally lift her off the ground and toss her lightly to one side. A shove up and away with the side of your foot is almost as effective. Now, before some readers start writing horrified letters, please bear in mind that I'm not advocating kicking or hurting your cat, but merely lifting her up and away from your legs and feet to show her that her actions aren't acceptable. The affront to her dignity and the sudden surprise of being lifted and tossed at the same time will probably make one or two lessons work.

I really don't think that you can be too severe about this. Even if you and your family are adept at dancing around your cat while retaining your balance, an unwitting visitor could easily become an accident victim because of it. Far better to have your cat associate surprise and shock with human feet and stay out of their way, than to have one or both of you seriously hurt.

2

Grooming

Why Cats Groom

Cats groom themselves all the time, for various reasons. Sometimes washing is used as a stalling device when a cat is embarrassed or unsure of what to do next. Grooming other cats and animals is usually a sign of affection and possession. But when a cat gives herself a thorough going-over, from head to toe, you can be sure that it's a real washing for cleanliness's sake. After completely grooming herself, a cat often preens and stretches, as if to say, "Admire me, I'm clean and beautiful." Praise from a fond human is expected and appreciated at this point.

Cats seem to be proud of their bodies and keep themselves tidy and clean all of the time. As a matter of fact, one of the surest signs that a cat is not feeling well is when she stops taking care of herself and forgets her daily grooming. A cat can be very distressed if something happens to make her look strange or unattractive. I can still remember what once happened to a cat named Peter.

When I was a child we lived in a house in the city. Some neighbors gave us a two-year-old silver long-haired neuter named Peter. Peter was one of the most beautiful cats I've ever seen outside of a show ring, with an exceptionally long, silky coat and a huge thick ruff of fur that stood out all around his neck. He was very placid, moved seldom in a deliberate fashion, and looked out at the world through round, impassive, pale yellow eyes. The only flicker of response to people that he ever showed was to purr loudly and vibrantly whenever anyone told him what a beautiful cat he was. He always stretched out in becoming places where he could be seen and admired, and invariably arranged himself artistically in a prominent spot when company came. Every day without fail, he "posed" for a few hours on the wide front living-room windowsill, where he could be seen and admired from the street. Passersby would sometimes actually ring our doorbell and ask about him. He seemed to understand, and to love it!

Peter had established a daily routine before he moved in with us. He would go out the back door into the fenced yard, jump up and proceed atop the adjoining fences to an opening into the street, and then stroll majestically, head up and tail waving like a flag, along the sidewalk around the city block we lived in. About an hour later, he'd appear on the front stoop to be let in. Despite this, he'd never worn a collar because of his enormous ruff.

One day, a lady who was new to the neighborhood saw him walking along the sidewalk, thought he was lost, and took him to her apartment. She immediately gave him a bath. Placid as always, Peter settled in with the lady, who kept him closed in and admired him a

Caring for Your Cat's Psyche

BASIC EQUIPMENT

Sturdy stiff-bristled brush
Fine-tooth comb
Towel or paper to cover grooming surface
Damp washcloth
Cotton swabs or Q-Tips

OPTIONAL EQUIPMENT

Vaseline, mineral oil, or other gentle lubricant
Cat nail clippers
Emery boards
Blunt-tipped scissors (especially for long-haired cats)
Tweezers
Cat flea powder
Gentle liquid shampoo or dry shampoo, made expressly for
    cats.

---

lot. About a week later, someone told us where Peter
was, and he was brought home, much to my delight
and his apparent indifference.

He seemed no worse for wear, but soon he developed a very severe infection in both ears from the
lady's bath water. The treatment was a messy one,
and the veterinarian had to shave all of the fur from
Peter's neck and head, giving him a comical pin-
headed appearance. Poor Peter couldn't stand it. He
found a niche in a dark corner of the cellar and
wouldn't come out. Long after the daily medication
sessions were over and the infections had cleared up,
he hid during the day and snuck outdoors to relieve
himself only under cover of darkness. It wasn't for
several more weeks, when his ruff had grown back
almost completely, that he finally came out, and
sometime later resumed his daily posings on the windowsill. We never understood how he knew what he

looked like, or sensed when his fur had grown back, but he did.

Grooming Your Cat

Most cats aren't nearly as vain as Peter, but they all seem to enjoy looking well and being admired. The amount and kind of grooming you'll want and need to do will vary a great deal according to the kind of cat you have and the life-style she leads. Owners of short-haired cats who keep themselves clean and neat will find that they have very little to do, while some long-hairs need daily care. But no matter how well your cat cares for herself, she should become accustomed to regular checkups. All cats learn to love being brushed and combed anyway, and a calm grooming session can be yet another pleasant expression of closeness and affection for both of you.

It sometimes annoys cat owners when their pets don't seem to trust them, but are wary about new procedures and grooming routines. Some cats will let their owners "do anything" to them; others always seem to fear the slightest new thing. It may help you to overcome your impatience with your nervous pet if you can put yourself in her place, remembering her size and inability to understand what you are doing. Cats will resist certain kinds of handling because they're afraid, or because they sense your nervousness and uncertainty about the procedure. Talking gently to your cat, or even singing if that's your thing, will help to reassure her that nothing bad is about to happen.

Know ahead of time exactly what you intend to do, and familiarize yourself with any equipment you'll be using. At the same time, let your cat get acquainted with the equipment. If you grab the cat and start to come at her with a strange object, such as metal clippers or a large hairbrush, it's no wonder that she's startled and frightened. Put the clippers down on the ground or near your cat's feeding dish and leave them there so that she can explore and sniff them thoroughly. Then pick them up and hold them lightly in your palm so that she can see and explore them there. After she's no longer afraid to approach the object in your hand, put your cat in her grooming place and move your hand and the object toward her. If she's still wary, let her sniff again. It may take awhile before a cat is sure enough to calmly let you use any new equipment on her, but if she's permitted to take her time, your cat will learn to trust you, and each new thing will be easier to introduce.

It will help if you can manage to groom the cat without any restraint. The idea is to make grooming a mutually pleasant and enjoyably experience, not a grim battle. Once your cat learns to trust you completely and accept your handling of her entire body, it will make any future kind of treatment, even medical procedures, less frightening and traumatic.

If your cat is particularly high-strung or active, however, you may need some kind of gentle restraint at first. It's better to hold her gently and firmly than to incite a terrifying chase around the house. A kitten or jumpy cat will usually feel secure and comfortable if you hold her in your lap.

WHEN AND WHERE

Unless you have a long-haired cat, or one who needs daily care for some particular reason, a weekly grooming is usually plenty. It's not necessary to have a set day or time; many owners simply seize an opportunity when both they and the cat are in the mood. Don't try to groom a cat when she's hungry or anxious to go out. Grown cats can usually be safely groomed after a meal, but too much handling right after eating can make a kitten throw up. If your cat is at all nervous or wild, the fewer distractions the better: other animals, small children, or any kind of frantic activity should be shut out of the room you're grooming in.

Because cats will always back away from something they're trying to avoid, the most escape-proof place to groom a cat is on your lap. It's also the best place to accustom a small kitten to being groomed, and the easiest spot to begin any strange or potentially frightening activity, such as clipping nails. Sitting in a chair with your lap protected, place your cat on your lap with her rear end against your middle. Holding her front legs in one hand from behind, use your free hand to start grooming.

After your pet is completely used to being groomed, you can switch to a table or countertop if you wish. Working on one of these surfaces can save your clothing, and they make it easier to keep any needed equipment handy. Cover the surface with a large towel or papers before lifting your cat up. Until your pet is familiar with this new spot and won't try to jump down, place one hand behind her rear end, or encircle her rear with an arm, bringing your hand around either to grasp her front legs or to rest on her chest.

BRUSHING AND COMBING

> Her white fur where she cleaneth it smells
> like talc.
> —EDWIN DENBY, "A Domestic Cat"

If cats groom themselves so well, what's the need of brushing and combing? There are several reasons why it's a good idea. Brushing is usually enjoyed by a cat, and it's a good first step toward other grooming routines that she may not like as well. At the same time, it gets rid of loose hair that would otherwise end up on your furniture or rugs, or in your cat's insides. It also provides an opportunity for a head-to-toe check of your pet's body for any kind of change or sign of trouble.

Long-haired cats usually need a lot of help taking care of their coats, and kittens should be trained to allow a thorough daily brushing and combing while their coats are still relatively thin and tangle-free. Otherwise, when they grow up they won't let you take proper care of their thick coats, which can then become matted and eventually will have to be clipped.

Even short-hairs that shed a great deal and have no help in removing loose fur will eventually ingest so much hair that it will form balls in their stomachs. They may be able to throw them up, but sometimes cats are unable to do so and have to have help in order to un-stop their innards (see p. 128).

If your pet goes outdoors, brushing and combing will help to get rid of dirt and odors. A good brushing with a dry shampoo will usually take the place of a wet bath when a cat has become very dirty.

In addition to all of these considerations, regular brushing and combing will stimulate your cat's circulation and natural skin oils, keep her skin healthy, her coat shiny, and make her feel and look sleek and well. Even almost hairless cats, such as the Rex, need and enjoy regular brushing.

Start as you did with stroking, along the top of your cat's head and back, with the growth of fur, from head to tail. That's the easy part, which almost all cats will enjoy. Work your way down on each side, again brushing the length of the cat. If fur accumulates in the brush, clean it out frequently. Under the chin is an-

45

other area that cats all enjoy having brushed. The stomach, under the front legs, and the rear thighs are often particularly sensitive, and many cats resist being brushed there. However, these are important areas in which to groom: it's in these spots that long-hairs most frequently become matted, and fleas and other parasites like these locations.

So you'll have to insist, gently but firmly, on brushing your cat's entire body, each time you groom. Don't let yourself be conned into brushing only where your pet wants you to. Automatically include the spots that are less appreciated by your cat as part of every grooming routine, and soon she'll learn to tolerate and accept being brushed all over, even if she never does learn to enjoy it all.

Be sure that you're not just skimming the surface as you brush, but are getting through to your cat's skin. If your pet has long fur, and there are mats or snarls, don't yank through them or just ignore them. Try to open and remove mats with a heavy comb. You may have to cut some out with blunt-tipped scissors. Then pay particular attention to those areas in future groomings so that mats don't form again.

After brushing your cat all over, go through her entire coat with a fine-tooth comb. This will remove dirt and loose hair, and help to locate any fleas, flea dirt, eggs, or larvae that your brush may have missed. Examine the towel or paper under your cat for fleas or specks: tiny black specks that will dissolve in water are flea feces, and are often mixed with little white eggs or tiny larvae, which are white or pale yellow and resemble fly maggots.

If your cat is particularly dirty or dusty, a damp terry cloth rubbed over his coat will get rid of the surface dirt before you start to brush. Rubbing with a damp cloth is also helpful as a last step, after brushing and combing, to remove any remaining loose hairs, and to calm down static electricity in your cat's fur created by brushing and combing.

Regular brushing and coming will usually clean even the dirtiest cat's coat. A dry, powdered shampoo made for cats can be used if your cat gets particularly dusty or dirty. But if your cat should get into something sticky, such as paint or gum, you'll have to remove it. If you can, cut the substance out with blunt scissors. If the affected area is too large to make this practical, or if it's in a relatively hairless spot such as a foot, try rubbing vegetable or mineral oil, or lard, into the sticky stuff and washing it off with a terry cloth. Don't ever use chemicals, such as paint remover, or cleaning fluid—remember that cats lick themselves all over. Sometimes it's necessary to leave the oil on overnight, with a wrapping to keep it in place. After this kind of treatment, you may have to bathe your cat.

Bathing

Most cats go through life without ever having a wet bath. Sometimes, however, there may be a situation in which a bath has to be given. Certain skin conditions can't be treated without medicated baths, for instance, or a cat may have got into something so foul that nothing short of a bath will help. There are also some cat owners who feel that their cats must be bathed regularly for either cosmetic or health reasons.

Unless you're one of those people who've accustomed their cats to regular baths, giving a cat a bath can be an extremely trying experience for both you and your pet. It's best to be well prepared, and to go through the routine as quickly and calmly as possible. Have all your equipment handy, including plenty of large towels. Unless you're using a medicated shampoo, choose a mild liquid castile soap made for babies, or a shampoo manufactured especially for cats. Never use detergent shampoo or bar soap—it will irritate a cat's eyes and skin. Creme rinses made just for cats will help you to comb out a long-haired coat.

Before bathing, protect your cat's ears with wads of lamb's wool. Cotton will do, but it absorbs water, while lamb's wool sheds moisture and protects better. Vaseline, mineral oil, or eye ointment, smeared around your cat's eyes, will protect them. Unless it's an emergency, and you don't have time, brushing your cat before the bath will remove loose hairs and help keep long coats from becoming more tangled when wet.

Choose a warm, draft-free room in which to bathe a cat. If your cat is not used to being bathed, she'll probably be very frightened and hard to handle. It's a great help to recruit a calm assistant, if possible. Hold the cat very firmly, with one hand grasping her front legs; you don't want to have a panicky chase, and your firm certainty will help to reassure your pet. Slippery porcelain surfaces will usually cause more struggling, so either use a plastic tub or line the bottom of your porcelain sink or tub with several layers of terry towels. Some handlers advocate putting a small window screen in the bottom of the tub for the cat to hang on to with her claws. If your cat is really hard to handle, you can put her in a small drawstring bag tied lightly around her neck, and bathe her, bag and all. This won't work if medication must go directly on your cat's skin, however.

Be sure that the water is warm and not too deep— use only enough to wet and rinse the cat completely. Don't try to use a spray hose or shower head, but pour the water over her with a cup or plastic container, or use a washrag to wet, but not soak, the cat. Rub the shampoo in thoroughly, and rinse by pouring water over the cat again. Be sure to remove all shampoo, and immediately wrap the animal in a large towel before removing her from the tub. Holding her close to you wrapped in a towel, rub her as much as you can, and reassure her before letting her down. If you bathe often, and start young enough, you may be able to accustom your cat to blow-drying, but most animals I know are terrified of the noise.

Old cats, sick cats, or kittens under six months should never be bathed unless your veterinarian feels that it's absolutely necessary.

Skin and Coat Problems

> The flea, though he kill none, he does all
> the harm he can.
> —JOHN DONNE, Devotion XII

What if you notice something wrong with your cat's skin or coat when you're brushing and combing her? If you see ticks or fleas you can probably treat them yourself, unless your pet is badly infested. Bare spots, lumps, rashes, red or rough areas will usually need expert diagnosis and treatment. Many skin conditions are hard to deal with, but almost all of them will respond to the proper treatment when it's given in time. Don't let anything odd go; the sooner any skin condition is arrested, the better.

Fleas are by far the most frequently found external parasites on cats, and, unless your cat is badly infested, they're often very hard for a novice to spot. Your first indication of fleas may be your pet's constant scratching. Some cats, however, seem not to be bothered by the itch too much until the fleas are really rampant, so don't count on scratching as a sign of them. Some cats have an allergic reaction to fleas, usually a rash on the stomach.

49

When you're brushing your cat, be particularly careful to examine her head and neck area, and under her front legs. When you turn her over on her back, riffle the stomach fur backward, so that you can see her skin. You may not see any fleas, but if you see small black specks, you can be pretty sure that there are fleas present. These small black specks are flea dirt. You can often spot these telltale signs on the towel or paper on which you groom your cat.

Fleas multiply fast, so waste no time in getting rid of them. It's best to check with your veterinarian first before using any powders or chemicals on your cat. He may recommend a dip or a good commercial flea powder or spray made for cats (don't use one meant for dogs, it will sicken your cat). Applied according to directions, this will usually get rid of the fleas. If your cat has an allergic rash, however, be sure to tell the doctor, since medication may be needed to clear it up.

Comb and brush your cat daily to get rid of the dead fleas. Eggs can be in bedding and surrounding areas, so wash, spray, and vacuum (throw away the bag!) anything your cat has come in contact with to prevent further infestation. Cat fleas can jump as far as three feet and are very adaptable, so don't overlook any part of the house your pet may have been in, especially cracks and crevices.

Once you've killed all the fleas on your pet, you'll want to take measures to prevent her from picking them up again, especially if she goes outdoors. Again, I recommend talking over what method to use with your doctor, because cats can be very sensitive to chemical substances. Some cats can tolerate flea collars, while others can develop skin irritations; flea tags sometimes work better. There are some home remedies for repelling fleas, such as feeding ½ teaspoon of brewer's yeast or other B vitamins daily, but I have had no firsthand experience with any of them. All these methods are designed only to repel fleas, not to kill any that are already on a cat, and none of them are foolproof, so it's still important to continue regular examinations of your pet for fleas.

Cats don't get ticks often, but if your pet frequents areas where ticks are likely to be found, such as woods or beach grasses, you may see an occasional tick on your cat. Ticks are small, dark-brown, hard-shelled, beetly-looking creatures with lots of legs. When they're engorged with blood they swell up and look like pale brown beans. They attach themselves to an animal's skin, usually around the head and neck area (under the collar) or between the toes, and they have to be pulled off with fingers or tweezers. The small red mark left on the cat's skin will heal by itself, but you can put a dab of antiseptic on it if you wish.

As I said before, other conditions such as flaking skin, bald patches, red spots, or rashes should be seen by a doctor for diagnosis. They could be caused by a number of things: parasites such as lice or mites that cause mange; allergies; dietary deficiencies; eczema; ringworm; or fungus. The treatment for these conditions varies considerably, and it's absolutely necessary to have professional help in order to clear them up.

Eyes and Ears

Some cats, especially those with long fur, seem to get goop in the corners of their eyes, which looks unsightly and sometimes mats the fur on the side of the nose. Holding your cat's head under the chin, gently remove any hard material with your fingertip or a tissue, and use a damp washcloth or cotton ball to wash off any remaining matter.

Cats' eyes should be clear and bright. Red or discolored whites can be a sign of illness. Irritation and/or illness can sometimes produce a strange-looking "film" over a cat's eyes. Actually, this is the third eyelid, which is usually hidden. If you notice it in only one eye, it's probably due to local irritation, such as something in the eye; if both eyes are affected, it may be owing to illness. If your pet seems otherwise healthy, and the "film" appears in only one eye, you probably needn't worry, and it will clear up in a few days. If you have any doubts, it's best to check with your veterinarian.

If you notice anything at all out of the ordinary about the insides of your cat's ears, they should be examined and treated. A healthy cat's ear is pink and somewhat shiny on the inside. If you see a brown, grainy substance, it's probably evidence of ear mites, which can lead to serious ear infections if left untreated. Unless you're sure the condition is mites, however, don't attempt to treat it yourself, since other conditions can be worsened by ear-mite medicine. Any kind of discharge or a foul odor is a sign of infection. Mineral oil rubbed gently on the inside skin of a cat's ear will provide temporary relief from itching, but you'll need a doctor's help to cure any ear disorder.

Pads and Claws

Look your cat's feet over when you're grooming her. Check between each toe pad for foreign objects, injuries, and parasites.

A cat who doesn't go outdoors at all will have to have her front claws clipped, because they'll grow too long without any abrasion. You may want to clip your cat's nails even if she does go out, to remove the sharp tips that catch on clothes and furnishings. If you've never clipped a cat's claws, I suggest that you have a veterinarian or professional animal groomer show you how to do it. It's really quite easy, once you have the knack and your cat's cooperation. Getting your cat used to this procedure as young as possible will help a great deal.

You can buy a professional cat-claw clipper, but human nail scissors or clippers are entirely satisfactory, for cat's claws are not very thick. Sit down, in a good light, and hold your cat in your lap with her back pressed against your middle. Since cats usually scratch only with their front claws, it isn't necessary to clip the back ones in order to protect your furniture; some owners do clip the back claws a little to protect themselves. Holding a front paw in your hand, press gently on the top and bottom until the claws extend. If your cat's claws are pale and transparent, the light will allow you to see just where the pink-colored "quick" ends. If her claws are dark and you can't see the quick, it's safe to assume that it ends just at the point where the claw starts to curve down. Holding the paw firmly, cut the point of the nail off, just below the quick. Follow this procedure with each nail and front paw. An emery board rubbed lightly over the cut ends of the claws will remove any loose or rough edges. If you should accidentally cut into the quick it will hurt, and it will probably bleed a little. You can stop the bleeding with a styptic pencil or daub of antiseptic, but you many have a little trouble convincing your cat that it won't happen again, so be careful.

Mouth and Teeth

Healthy teeth and gums are essential to a cat's continued well-being as she gets older, and yet they're often neglected by cat owners. There's really no need for this, because it's very simple to check your cat's mouth regularly, and early preventive treatment of any disorders can help avoid expensive painful dental work later on.

In the course of your regular grooming, grasp your cat's chin in one cupped hand, and force her mouth open by pushing firmly on both sides of the "hinges" of her jaw. With your free hand, move her tongue to one side so that you can see under it, as things can get lodged there. Kittens often swallow a string or thread, and part of it may remain stuck under the tongue. If you can't remove it by gentle pulling, it could be knotted inside the cat somewhere, or a needle might be embedded in her insides, and only a doctor can remove it safely.

Use your thumb to push your cat's lips back so that you can see her teeth and gums. Healthy gums are pink and firm; pale gums are abnormal. Run a finger along the gums, pushing slightly. Bleeding of the gums may indicate the beginning of disease. If your cat's gums look all right, but bleed slightly when they're rubbed, you can help restore them to health by keeping her teeth clean and massaging her gums regularly. If the gums continue to bleed, you should let your veterinarian take a look to determine the cause. You'll also need a doctor's help if you notice any lumps, lesions, or loose teeth.

Just as with people, the propensity to develop tartar varies with individual cats. Some cats accumulate a great deal of tartar on their teeth. Others, who regularly chew on hard things, may never have much. Excessive tartar buildup can cause gum disease and the eventual loss of teeth, so it's important not to ignore it. If you accustom your cat to the routine early, you can clean her teeth. With a wet terry cloth or gauze pad wrapped around your index finger, vigorously rub the surface of each tooth. This will help remove slimy film, but it usually won't remove tartar that has already formed. You can often take off light tartar deposits with your fingernail, but if they've built up for some time, you may have to have your cat's teeth cleaned with special instruments. After a professional cleaning, you can keep tartar down with regular maintenance.

Something hard to chew on daily will help to keep your cat's teeth clean. Accustom your pet to eating some dry food or chewing on a large dog biscuit.

Extras and Adornments

A healthy, clean cat has very little odor. Most cats I've known have had a delightful, faint talcum-powder smell. So I can see no merit in the various sprays and liquid cat "perfumes" on the market. Nor, I imagine, do most cats. If your cat smells bad, she's either sick or needs a bath; unless, of course *he's* an unaltered tom, and I don't think that even the strongest perfume could make a real tomcat smell like anything except what he is.

I feel the same way about all artificial adornments for cats, such as fancy ribbons, jeweled collars, and so forth. Cats are beautiful creatures and neither need nor care for gimmicky adornments.

Two useful extras, however, are a harness and a collar. If you have an indoor cat and want to train her to walk on a leash, you'll need a harness. I won't argue about whether it's "natural" for a cat to walk on a leash, because when they're trained to it young, many cats seem to enjoy this activity, and it can certainly be convenient if you plan to travel with your pet at all.

Cats are more comfortable in a harness than in a

collar when they are walking on a leash, and they can't slide out of it easily. You'll have to measure your cat's girth for a proper fit. Choose a lightweight, elasticized harness for optimum comfort, and get your cat used to wearing it in gradual stages before you attempt to walk her in it. Practice with a leash indoors until your cat will walk instead of lying down.

The first few times you venture outside, bring along your carrier, since cats are often terrified by street noises, and you can pop your pet into the carrier if she becomes frantic. Calm reassurance and frequent short trips should eventually accustom even the scarediest cat to walking on a leash.

Some people won't put any kind of collar on a cat, for fear that it will get caught on something and choke her. I feel that a reflecting collar with an identifying tag is an absolute necessity for a cat who is allowed outdoors alone. The benefits of wearing a collar far outweigh any possible danger, and my cats have always worn collars. If the collar is loose enough and also elasticized, a cat can pull her head right through if she gets stuck. Several of my cats have done just that and come home collarless. A cat who roams can be hurt or get closed in someone's garage or cellar. If she's not wearing a tag, you'll never know what happened to her. In addition, a reflecting collar or tag can help her to be seen by drivers.

Measure your cat's neck, and choose a lightweight collar that will allow two of your fingers, on edge, to fit between your cat's neck and the collar. Most cat collars are now either made entirely of elastic, or have a strip or two of elastic on either side of the buckle.

If your cat or kitten has never worn a collar before, you'll have to get her used to it gradually. Most cats will try to get the collar off right away; when they can't succeed with their front paws, they'll try to bite it off.

The results are that they often get their bottom jaws caught under the collar, or their bottom teeth stuck in the buckle. The first time this happened to one of my kittens, I couldn't imagine what was the matter with him, as he ran wildly around in circles, howling, his chin pressed down onto his chest. If you can't undo the collar because the cat's teeth are stuck in the buckle, you may have to cut it off. Usually cats learn from this experience, and don't attempt to dislodge the collar again. But, until you're sure that your pet won't become entangled in a collar, put it on only when you're around to watch her. Soon she'll become so accustomed to wearing it she won't even seem to notice.

One further word about collars. The elastic in cat collars has a limited life span. After about a year, it either stretches so much that the collar falls off, or it stiffens and hardens and looses it elasticity. Since cat collars are very inexpensive, you can replace a worn one painlessly.

3

Entertainment and Exercise

What fun to be a cat!
— CHRISTOPHER MORLEY,
"In Honour of Taffy Topaz"

Cats are never too young or too old to enjoy playing, either by themselves or with you. The right toys can entertain even the liveliest kitten, and playing will not only provide needed exercise for muscles and teeth, but can also help to keep an energetic young cat out of trouble by tiring her out and distracting her from mischief. Encouraging an older cat to play, even for just a few minutes a day, can help her circulation, appetite, and general health to improve, and will prevent stiffening up of her aging joints and muscles.

Some cats are naturally very active. These really "hyper," clownish cats will tumble around and race from room to room with little, if any, encouragement. Others are more sedentary. Peter, for instance, was a very dignified cat and hardly seemed to be the playing type but once in a while, when he thought no one was watching, we'd spot him pouncing out at something and tumbling wildly over and over around it. As soon as he sensed that he was being watched, he'd get up and stalk away, shaking his back legs, as if to say, "That wasn't me!"

No matter how comic your cat may be, there's one thing that you should bear in mind whether you're playing with her or watching her play by herself. You must never laugh at a cat or make her look foolish or awkward. All cats need to be allowed to retain their dignity, and they really have no sense of humor about themselves. You may not take this seriously, but you'll find that if you make fun of your cat, or laugh at her too much, she'll become upset and won't play or romp with you for quite a long time. If your cat somehow manages to upend herself when she's playing, and falls ungracefully to the floor on her head, try not to laugh. Pretend that you didn't see, and give your pet time to right herself. Usually, when a cat does anything she's ashamed of, such as falling or knocking something over clumsily, she'll first look around to see if anyone noticed, and then she'll get up and walk away stiffly, head up. After going a few steps, she'll then shake her hind legs one by one, as if to rid herself of the offending act. Often she'll turn her head and look over her shoulder scornfully, seeming to say, "What stupid oaf did that unseemly thing?" It's almost as if cats think that, by pretending they haven't done something foolish, they can eradicate it.

On a more practical note, active, playful cats should always have their claws well trimmed. Trimmed claws will inflict less damage on toys and on you, should you get in the way. More important, if you remove the sharp hooked tips of your cat's claws, she's less likely to catch them and wrench her leg or hurt herself trying to get loose.

Entertainment

Some toys and playthings are more fun when there's a person around to help a cat play with them, but there are a number of items with which a kitten or cat can entertain herself.

THE RIGHT KINDS OF TOYS

Toys for cats need to be carefully selected: in order to serve their purpose they must be both practical and safe. For example, toys meant to be carried or batted around have to be light enough; thus, while a hard-rubber ball may be perfectly safe, it's probably too heavy for your kitten to handle, and she'll quickly lose interest in it. There are a few basic safety rules that you should remember when you buy, or make, toys for your cat:

- Anything you give your cat to play with should be too big for her to possibly swallow.
- Toys for cats must be too hard to be chewed into pieces. Brittle plastic, Styrofoam, and soft rubber can all be easily torn to bits.
- Watch out for bells, squeakers, and rattles in toys—kittens especially can get at them with ease.
- The strings on dangling or hanging toys should be very securely attached at both ends, so that the end can't work loose and be swallowed, or wind around a cat's neck.
- Watch out for things that can splinter, like wood and some bones.
- Metal toys may have sharp edges—besides, cats don't much like metal.
- Be sure that anything your cat plays with is colored with nontoxic paint.

Caring for Your Cat's Psyche

Most of these rules are simply common sense, but if you've never owned a cat before, you might not realize just how strong and sharp cats' teeth and claws can be, and how quickly they can rip things apart when they're determined. Most toys intended for children won't withstand a cat's sharp teeth and claws.

"Found" Toys and Toys Easy to Make

You really don't need to rush out and buy toys for your cat. There are a number of "found" items probably lying around your house that your cat will like to play with. You can also make many simple playthings out of household items.

One of the things that can provide hours of entertainment for all cats, no matter how old they are, is a crumpled-up piece of cellophane. This paper has the wonderful characteristic of slowly "moving" when it's been crumpled into a tight ball, and cats find it endlessly exciting to pounce on, bat, and carry around. Watch to be sure that your cat doesn't start to chew the cellophane and swallow bits of it. The same precaution applies to pipe cleaners, which make great toys but have to be taken away as soon as your pet begins to chew on them.

A plain pencil is fun for a cat to play with. She'll toss it in the air, leap out at it, bat it around, and even carry it from here to there. The only problem with pencils is that you don't want your cat to chew on them when she gets bored with playing and get bits of paint, wood, eraser, or lead in her mouth. So take the pencil away when you're not around.

A walnut in its shell makes a wonderful "ball" for a cat; so does a large, empty, wooden spool.

Cardboard paper-towel or toilet-paper rolls are very amusing.

Big corks strung together can either be suspended from a doorknob to be batted around, or dragged along the floor by a willing human to make a good pounce toy.

An old white athletic sock, knotted, is excellent for a cat to chew on. So is a large knucklebone, boiled to kill any parasites.

All cats love to get into things, and an empty paper bag, placed on the floor, will keep your cat busy for hours. She'll go in and out of the bag, tumble over inside it, jump on it, and usually wind up curling up inside it and going to sleep.

No cat can resist an empty carton or box either. Put a box on the floor, and your cat will hop in and out of it, explore every corner of it, and then lie down or sit in it for a while. A cat-sitter we once had in the city taught us how to make a maze, or house, for a cat by stacking several cardboard cartons on top of each other in a pyramid, cutting holes at random in adjoining sides or tops and bottoms, and creating a whole labyrinth for a cat to play in. Taping the boxes together with masking tape will prevent the whole thing from tumbling down when your cat gets carried away with her new toy.

Even if you have only the most basic sewing skills, you can create a number of different toys for your cat out of scraps. For instance, you can take two heavy pieces of cloth, such as felt or burlap, sew them together on three sides, turn the whole thing inside out, stuff it with catnip, stitch the remaining open side firmly with an over-and-over stitch, and you've made a catnip "mouse"! (Believe me, your cat won't know the difference.)

If you're really crafty, you can crochet or knit toys for your cat, filling the centers with lightweight Wiffle balls or crumpled-up paper and some catnip. And, if your sewing skills are more advanced, you can make other stuffed toys for your pet. Remember not to stuff your cat's toys with anything you don't want her to eat, however; she may not respect your fine workmanship and will probably tear her new toys apart.

Leftover yarn pieces or scraps of carpeting can be tied tightly together in the center and trimmed to make a light toy that a cat can carry around easily.

The number of things you can make for your cat to play with is limited only by your imagination and skill. If you have neither the time, inclination, nor the patience to create toys for your cat, there are an endless number of items you can buy for her.

Toys to Buy

Pet stores, department stores, and even supermarkets usually carry a wide array of cat toys. Many of the catnip toys I see for sale, though, aren't really safe: a lot of them have bells or rattles inside them, and it's impossible to tell if they're big enough to be swallowed. Some also have decorations made of bits of cloth lightly stitched on the outside, which could easily come loose and be swallowed. Usually, the simpler the toy the safer it is; things such as woolen balls and unadorned catnip mice are best.

Lightweight plastic Wiffle balls with holes in them make excellent toys. The plastic they're made of is soft enough so that it won't splinter, and the holes make them easy for a cat to carry around.

Ping-Pong balls are fun for a cat to play with, too, but when they get broken, they have sharp edges that can cut a cat's mouth. If your cat's a chewer, take Ping-Pong balls away from her when you're not around.

Spring toys that can be mounted on the top of a

scratching post or other stationary object are great fun for a cat to play with. Remember that they must be very firmly attached and, again, they should have no parts that might come loose and be swallowed.

Toys to hang from doorknobs, drawer pulls, or posts can be strung on elastic. The problem is that when elastic gets old, it can break very easily and a cat could get a piece of it caught in her throat or wound around her neck—so check the elastic and replace it if needed.

Mostly for Exercise

There are also all kinds of equipment you can buy or make for your cat that not only will provide entertainment, but will give her an opportunity for very good exercise.

The best of these is a long carpet-covered pole with "landings" on it, known variously as a cat tree, pole house, climbing tree, or exercise pole. The design varies quite a bit: many consist of a metal tension pole, mounted on a flat carpet-covered board about a yard square, which fits snugly between the floor and ceiling. The pole is always covered with carpeting, so that a cat can get her claws into it to climb up. There are several "landings" attached, with holes cut next to the pole for the cat to get through. The "landings" are also covered with carpet. Some are all simply flat platforms, while others have some box-shaped sections with additional holes cut out in their sides. Usually, these poles are designed to fit into the corner of a room so that the walls can provide added support on two sides when a cat plays on the pole and platforms.

Other types of exercise or climbing trees are made to hang over the top of a door—these are useful if you have limited space and don't want to give up a corner.

There are also pieces of cat-climbing apparatus consisting of several stacking units, so that you can have just the height your own room will accommodate. Once you've seen one of these climbing trees, you may decide to make one yourself out of a tension pole, wood, and carpeting, or you can simply stack wooden boxes and cover them with carpet. Commercial trees range in price from about $30 to $90, depending on how elaborate they are, and they're available in pet stores and through pet suppliers. Although they're expensive, a well-made climbing tree should last your pet for her entire life, so you might consider it a good investment.

These poles can't be beaten as outlets for energy, especially for an energetic cat who spends all her time indoors. Randolph and Patrick, two very active young Rex cats who never go out, spend hours running up and down their tree, chasing each other. They carry toys up to the various levels in their mouths, drop them, go down and fetch them, and carry them up again, and invent all kinds of other games to play alone or with each other, all revolving around their tree. These two often sleep on the top level, too, in a beanbag bed. Their owner says she'd hate to think of the mischief they'd get into if they didn't have their tree to play on.

There are other kinds of carpeted exercise contraptions that are less elaborate. One of the items I've seen for sale takes advantage of cats' love for getting into things. It's a carpeted "play tunnel"—a round tube, about nine to ten inches in diameter and two feet long, covered with carpet, and mounted lengthwise on a flat board or stand. Some have a spring toy attached at one end, hanging over the tunnel opening. These tunnels retail for about $20. It would be quite easy to create a similar toy by making a foot-square wooden box about

65

two feet long, open at both ends, mounting it horizontally on a base, and covering the whole thing with carpet. Putting some catnip underneath the covering before attaching it would make your "tunnel" even more attractive to your cat.

A window perch covered with carpet is another item sold in many stores. While these supply no exercise, they do provide entertainment, giving a housebound cat a comfortable place on which to sit and look out of the window. They consist simply of a foot-wide length of carpet-covered wood, designed to rest on top of a windowsill and extend over the edge. The perch is supported by a diagonal "arm" from its bottom edge to the wall below at an angle of about forty-five degrees.

These are the most frequently seen kinds of climbing and exercise devices made for cats, but there are undoubtedly more, and you can probably invent others yourself if you wish. Just be sure that any exercise or climbing equipment that you buy or make for your cat is sturdy enough not to topple over under her full weight and enthusiasm, and well enough made not to come apart with vigorous use.

Games to Play with Your Cat

> When I play with my cat, who knows whether I do not make her more sport than she makes me?
> —MICHEL DE MONTAIGNE,
> *Essays*, Book II, chap. 12

Play is an important aspect of your relationship with your pet. A young kitten's natural energy and liveliness can provide hours of entertainment and amusement for you. But, though it's fun just to watch a kitten or cat bounce and leap around, it can do a great deal to cement the bond between you if you join in the play sometimes. If your kitten doesn't have another cat or kitten to play with, you can help her to indulge in play activities—necessary for her to develop fully, both physically and emotionally, according to animal behaviorists.

If you watch two cats playing with each other, or even a cat playing alone with a toy, you'll notice that there are several actions cats almost always use in play. They stalk, pounce, carry, toss, bat with their paws, jump in the air, and sometimes chase things—all of which are basically natural hunting or fighting motions.

Any games that you invent to play with your cat should make use of one or more of these instinctive feline actions. One game, for instance, that is very entertaining for any cat is "pounce." All that's required of you is to pull an object along the floor in front of your pet so that she can jump out and grab it. A long string or piece of yarn is the best thing for this game, because it ensures that your hand will be well out of reach of your pet's grasping claws. If you use something short like a pencil, protect your hand with a glove; constantly interrupting the game by reminding your cat about "velvet paws" is likely to spoil it. Variations on this game can be developed by jerking the string up in the air a foot or so just as your cat reaches it, so that she'll have to leap to get it.

Another kind of pounce all cats enjoy is "hidden object pounce." This game requires that something thin and flat, such as a newspaper, magazine, piece of paper, sweater, or blanket be lying on a hard surface like the floor or a tabletop. (Note: If you use a paper or magazine for this game, be sure that it's something you no longer care about.) Slide a pencil, ruler, or other long sticklike object (not your hand!) under the edge of the paper, and move it around. Your cat will immediately pounce, and then sit back, surprised, because there's nothing there to get her claws into. This can happen several times until she finally figures out that whatever's moving is under the covering, and then goes under herself to investigate.

Hiding a toy or ball underneath something lightweight can give your cat an intriguing puzzle to solve, too. Once she retrieves the object, don't be surprised if she hides it again herself, or brings it to you to be rehidden.

Going under or into things is another game cats enjoy. Try putting a piece of newspaper or a paper bag over your cat when she's on the floor. This will be a signal for her to play hide-and-seek in it, go on top of it, all around it, back under it, and generally have a good time, while destroying the paper or bag. Wilbur recently developed a variation of this game with a rather thin, old scatter rug in the bathroom. I came in to find him under the rug, peeking out, and as I watched he rolled himself up in the edge of the rug, came out, lifted up another edge, and burrowed headfirst underneath again, sat there for a few minutes, and finally came out again—all the while purring furiously.

Cats also love to chase small objects that they can pick up once they catch them. This is a very good game for exercise. Lightweight Wiffle balls, paper or yarn balls, catnip mice, or other small toys make excellent "fetch" objects. With some patient repetition, you can probably teach your cat to bring the object back to you to be retossed for a while until she tires of the game and carries off the toy to play with by herself.

Batting things is another favorite cat activity. You can get into the game by dangling and swinging something for your cat to hit at—just a simple piece of string or yarn will do, but tying a crumpled ball of paper or a light toy on the end of the cord will make it more fun for your cat.

If your cat's very energetic, and you'd like to tire her out a bit, you can chase her around the house, up and down stairs, or into rooms and behind doors. This works for some cats who enjoy it, but it can affect others badly, making them become hysterically wild. You'll have to judge for yourself whether this is a good form of play for your cat to indulge in. If your cat should become overwrought after a vigorous play session, talk to her calmly and stroke her soothingly. As I mentioned in Chapter 1 in the section on "crazy fits," cats will usually calm down and go to sleep when left alone.

SPONTANEOUS GAMES

Opportunities for spontaneous games can often come up in the course of normal household living. If you have the time and inclination, you can turn these moments into the occasion for some fun with your cat.

Most kittens really like to "help" when you're making a bed. They'll crouch under the covers and leap out at your hand, and let themselves be "made" into the bed, sitting in a lump under the tucked-in covers until you provide an escape hole.

Open dresser drawers are a cat's delight. I've never left a drawer open for more than a moment without a cat jumping in, and either curling up and going to sleep, or thoroughly exploring as far back as possible, and sometimes even climbing down into the drawer below if there's room.

Any time that you have a package to unwrap, let your cat join in the fun, too—nothing pleases a kitten or even a grown cat more than getting involved with wrappings and boxes.

Some cats are intrigued with dripping water. A faucet left on just enough so that it drips slightly can amuse some cats for an amazingly long time, watching and patting at the drip.

There are times when a cat just can't resist putting a paw out to grab a moving pencil or pen. If you stop and play for a few minutes, your pet will probably go away satisfied, but if you try to ignore her and go on with your work, she'll probably persist until you either lose patience with her or give in and play anyway.

Some owners get annoyed when their young kittens start to make a game out of every household job. Kittens who continually make it impossible to finish any task may be indicating to their owners that they're not receiving enough attention or playtime. Others may simply be too full of high spirits to allow an opportunity for play to go by. Whatever the reason, taking a few minutes out to play with your cat on the spur of the moment will not only delight her, but will help to make her into an outgoing, spontaneous cat who's able to respond to you openly and with enthusiasm when you want her to.

Tricks to Teach Your Cat

Cats aren't usually known for their ability to learn tricks. In general, they don't respond readily to voice commands the way dogs do, for instance. But everyone's seen trained lions and tigers, so it's obvious that cats *can* be taught to do tricks.

If you want to astound your dog-loving friends, or if you just think that it might be fun to do, you can teach your cat to do certain kinds of "tricks" fairly easily. I put the word in quotation marks, because these things aren't really tricks at all, but perfectly natural actions your cat can learn to do on cue. Some breeds of cat are said to be particularly easy to teach, by the way—Siamese, for instance, are supposed to be very quick studies—but I've found that most fairly intelligent cats can be taught some basic "tricks."

Wilbur has a "trick" that often amazes visitors. When it's his dinner time, precisely at six o'clock, he paces up and down the counter where he's fed, waiting for his meal. As he paces, he often rubs against an electric can opener on the counter, making it turn on with a whirring sound. Since this is the machine with which his canned meal is opened, people often assume that he associates the sound of the motor with dinner, and is hinting none too subtly for speed. I'm sure that the whole thing is just coincidence, and if a toaster was on the counter rather than a can opener, he'd rub on that instead. I could easily turn this routine into a real "trick," however, by saying "Turn on the can opener, Wilbur," at the appropriate moment. A lot of cats regularly turn their bowls over when they're empty—another "trick."

There are many kinds of "tricks" like this that you can teach your cat to do. One easy thing to teach most cats is to "fetch." By showing your pet that you'll toss an object again for her if she brings it back, she'll soon learn to return it on command. Often the fun of playing with you is enough reward for a cat to learn to "fetch," but if it's not, a food reward and praise every time she returns a toy will soon help your cat to learn this "trick."

Many cats habitually answer you when you speak to them. If your pet is at all vocal, you can teach her to "speak" when spoken to by praising and rewarding her every time she responds to certain words. Other

71

actions can be turned into "tricks"—cats who frequently kiss, for instance, can be taught how to show affection on command by a patient owner.

If your cat regularly rolls over onto her back when you start to stroke her in a certain spot, you can combine a vocal command with the physical action. Soon, if she really likes to have her tummy rubbed, she'll probably learn to react to your voice alone and will "roll over" on cue.

Once you've established a relationship with your cat that includes her being able to respond to some simple vocal commands, you can go on to harder tricks if you wish. Be sure that she's old enough to pay attention when you want her to, and not to be too easily distracted. There are some basic steps involved in training any animal to learn something. First, you have to show her what you want her to do as simply as possible. If you want her to jump up on a certain spot on a counter, for instance, you have to put her onto that spot, at the same time saying "Up," or "Jump," or whatever. A one-word command is best—too many words can be confusing. Second, you must repeat both the words and the action a number of times. Your cat's attention span may not permit too many lessons in one session; as soon as she obviously tires of the whole thing, or starts to protest, stop and don't resume again until the next day. Third, you should reward her with lavish praise and a food treat if she even seems to be catching on. If she jumps up correctly once, for example, and then loses track of what she's supposed to be doing the second time, you should still praise her. Don't get cross with your cat or scold her if she doesn't seem to understand; this will only confuse her and make her associate something unpleasant with the whole thing.

If your initial efforts are successful, you may decide

to try some tricks that aren't based mostly on a cat's natural abilities and actions, such as "sit and stay," or "beg." It's wise to remember, though, before you get carried away, that no animal can do any trick that is beyond her physical strength, agility, or concentration span, so don't try to make your cat do something too difficult for her. You'll only make her miserable.

SECTION TWO

Caring for Your Cat's Physique

She is feeling well, because her eyes are clear and her coat is smooth.
—FRANCES AND RICHARD LOCKRIDGE,
Cats and People

4

Pleasing Your Cat's Palate

But the kittens were rude, and grabbed
their food.

—JOSEPH GREEN FRANCIS,
"A Little Girl Asked Some Kittens to Tea"

Kittens seem to eat a great deal for their size. I remember one of my children asked me once why a kitten we had didn't get fat because he ate so much. The reason for this seemingly too-large appetite is that cats have very high protein and fat requirements, which means that their caloric intake has to be relatively large in order to supply these needs. In general, healthy cats who are given a balanced diet don't ever overeat and won't get fat. On the other hand, if you're feeding your cat a diet that doesn't contain enough protein, fat, and other important dietary elements, then she may consume excessively large quantities of food in an effort to get the proper nutrition, and she'll get fat from all of those extra calories.

Cats are particularly apt to form strong diet preferences; hence the myth of the finicky cat. These conditioned food preferences usually don't represent a complete, nutritious diet, however; so you can't rely on your cat to know enough to eat right. Nor should you assume that just any cat food you buy will supply

---

SOME GENERAL FEEDING GUIDELINES

1. Feed your cat regularly, or leave food out where she can get it. Don't ever make a cat beg for her food.
2. Feed adult cats at least twice a day.
3. Accustom your cat to eating a variety of foods early in life.
4. Don't give dog food to cats. It doesn't meet their requirements.
5. Give cat food at room temperature.
6. Cook fresh meat and fish lightly to destroy parasites.
7. Always provide plenty of fresh drinking water.
8. Provide something hard to chew on for healthy teeth and gums, but don't give bones that might splinter, and don't feed unsoftened dry food to kittens under six months.
9. Don't give dietary supplements without consulting your veterinarian.
10. If your cat vomits frequently, or is "off her feed" for more than twenty-four hours, contact your veterinarian.

---

the proper nourishment. You should base your cat's diet on your own knowledge and judgment.

In order to feel well and respond to you, a cat needs a diet that meets all of her needs. A poorly fed cat isn't a very satisfactory pet. Although many of the results of an improper diet won't surface for years, there are often some immediate effects you might not necessarily associate with poor nutrition. Hypersensitivity, crankiness, lethargy, listlessness, and a dull, rough coat that sheds a lot are some of the more obvious signs that your cat may not be eating right. If your pet exhibits any of these characteristics, you should suspect a nutritional deficiency. Talk to your veterinarian about your cat's diet before you assume that you must have a disappointing, unresponsive pet.

It's no wonder that cat owners are often confused or uncertain as to just what does constitute a proper feline diet. No other area of cat well-being has had more mythology and misinformation surrounding it in the past. Until less than a generation ago, no research at all had been done into cats' specific nutritional needs. Even now there are some recognized necessary dietary elements for which no minimum daily requirements have been set for cats. However, a great deal of research in the area of feline nutrition is now being done. Some of this research is funded, if not actually performed, by several of the major pet-food manufacturers.

Here are some of cats' general nutritional needs that these researchers agree on:

- Cats need a variety of foods in order to meet their nutritional requirements. (You don't have to think up a new taste thrill daily, but you should provide several different *kinds* of food each day.)
- Cats have an extremely high daily protein and fat requirement. Foods designed for dogs and/or humans don't meet their needs.
- Despite former beliefs, cats should have some carbohydrates in their daily diet.
- Fresh drinking water is essential to a cat's well-being. Depriving a cat of plenty of water, or assuming that she'll meet her water requirement through food, is a major mistake.

When and Where to Feed Your Cat

Kittens have to eat twice as much food per pound of weight as adult cats. Since kittens' stomachs are very small, they must either have food available all the time, so that they can eat at will, or else you'll have to feed them small meals four or five times a day. As your kitten grows and her capacity increases, you can cut down the number of daily feedings while increasing the portions, until you're finally able to feed her the equivalent of two meals a day when she's full-grown. (See Tables 1 and 2, pages 96 and 99, for approximate calories and portions.) Even grown cats, however, are unable to consume enough at one time to meet their daily needs; that's why cats are often referred to as "occasional" eaters. Cats rarely overeat, so you can pretty much feed your adult cat all that she'll take in one sitting, or allow her continuous access to food throughout the day.

I prefer to feed my grown cats one proper, scheduled meal daily, and to leave some dry food in a bowl for snacking during the day (or night). There are several reasons why it's desirable to have at least one regular mealtime for a cat. If your pet goes outdoors, checking in at dinner time is a good routine to establish, especially if you have more than one cat. Cats like to know when they're going to be fed, and will always appear right on time. Serving a meal on schedule enables you to observe your cat's appetite or lack of it, and it also provides an opportunity to give any needed medication, treatment, or diet additive and be sure that it's taken. By the way, though, try not to be too rigid in your timing, because if you're out or delayed for some reason, your cat will think you've deserted her. It's also a good idea to accustom your cat to being fed by more than one family member so that she doesn't become too dependent.

Where you feed your cat isn't particularly important, as long as you're consistent. Cats are creatures of habit and will automatically go to the same place to be fed. Some cats are so set in their ways that they won't eat in a spot other than the one they're accustomed to. Besides, having her "own" eating spot will discourage your cat from trespassing on yours.

FEEDING DISHES

You really don't need any special, or fancy, dishes on which to feed your cat. Any clean plate will do. Because of their keen sense of smell, cats often won't eat from an unwashed plate—besides which, it's insanitary.

Flat plates or dishes are best for feeding moist canned foods. Cats don't like to stick their faces into a bowl of wet food and if they're fed in a deep bowl, they'll often take bites of food out with a paw. On the other hand, a bowl with high sides is best for dry or semimoist food that you leave out all day. This will help prevent excessive spilling, even though your cat may still remove pieces of food with her paw. If you're leaving a bowl of dry food on a high place, such as a kitchen chair or counter, be sure that it's weighted or heavy enough not to slide or be knocked over the edge.

I don't especially like the double cat bowls that are sold all over. They're harder to keep clean than single bowls, and it seems as if the contents of the two bowls are always getting mixed up. Although I've never encountered this problem, some cats are apparently allergic to plastic dishes and will break out in a rash on their chins or faces. If you want to use a plastic dish or water bowl, watch your cat for a week or two for signs of this allergy. The other problem with even the high-impact plastic is that it eventually becomes hard to clean, and odors and stains seem to permeate the plastic. Of course, you can always discard a plastic bowl that has become discolored or smelly, but ceramic seems better in the long run. Metal dishes are all right for food and are easy to clean, but some will eventually "pock" when water stands in them.

Cats' Nutritional Needs

While what follows may seem difficult and complicated to you, you don't need to worry unduly about it. The most important thing to remember is that if you feed your cat a variety of good foods, you'll undoubtedly provide her with all of the nutrients essential to health. The main reason that I'll go into the details of proper feline nutrition is so that you can be aware of some harmful lacks and excesses, most of which are created only when a cat is fed an exclusive, or almost exclusive, diet of just one food or type of food, rather than a variety.

There are only a few special circumstances in which you should really concern yourself with detailed feeding requirements. Certain illnesses can deplete a cat's reserves of some nutrients very quickly. If a cat has a long bout of diarrhea, for instance, some of the vitamins normally found in her intestines may be lacking. High fever, antibiotics, or other digestive upsets may destroy or prevent the synthesis, or absorption, of other necessary nutrients. Very old age, pregnancy, and nursing are some other special circumstances that may require particular attention to diet. These conditions may call for supplementation of some sort, but be sure to check with your veterinarian before giving any. It's important that any supplements are in the correct proportions, or they may do more harm than good.

Here's a brief general summary of the range of nutritional needs of an average cat, which can provide rough feeding guidelines.

PROTEIN

Protein is the single most important element in a cat's daily diet. Cats need two or more[1] times as much protein as dogs do each day. An adult cat's diet should be approximately 25 to 35 percent protein, depending on her activity level.

The important thing to know about protein is that it's made up of twenty-two different amino acids, at least ten of which are called "essential" because they're not manufactured within a cat's body and must be replenished each day. Not all proteins contain all of these essential amino acids. Vegetables, for instance, do not provide all of them unless they are supplemented. Meat, fish, poultry, and eggs are the best sources of protein for cats.

It has been known for some time that a lack of taurine, one of the two essential amino acids that cats cannot manufacture in their own bodies (arginine is the other), could cause retinal damage and eventual blindness in cats, and retard the growth of kittens[2]. In 1987, however, studies revealed that insufficient dietary taurine could also cause a cat to develop *dilated cardiomyopathy* (DCM), a disease in which the heart muscle becomes flabby and weak and its pumping action is reduced.[3] The major pet-food manufacturers have responded to this new finding quickly, and now formulate their diets with sufficient taurine. Taurine supplements are usually not necessary and shouldn't be given except under a veterinarian's supervision.

CARBOHYDRATES

Carbohydrates are more likely to be left out of a cat's diet than protein is. For many years, experts thought that cats needed few, if any, carbohydrates, and there are still no established minimum daily carbohydrate requirements for cats.

In the wild, however, when a cat catches prey, the first thing that she usually eats are the innards. Even domestic cats who don't entirely consume the small rodents or birds that they kill will often eviscerate their catch and eat the internal organs. Since feline prey is vegetarian, there is always some partially digested plant matter left in the stomach and intestines.

It stands to reason, then, that if a cat gets no vegetable matter in her diet, she's missing something. Starch, which is present to a greater or lesser degree in all plants, is well utilized by cats when it's cooked. (The starch in raw vegetables won't be absorbed and will often cause diarrhea.) Carbohydrates also provide useful calories and bulk and release the proteins in other food sources so that they can go to work in more complex ways within a cat's body.

Most commercial cat foods have some vegetable matter cooked into them, usually grains, potatoes, or beans, particularly soybeans. Many cats also enjoy an occasional treat of fresh-cooked vegetables, such as green beans or corn. If you feed your cat only home-prepared foods, include some cooked vegetables daily, either whole or ground and mixed into her food. Non-vegetable sources of carbohydrates are sweets and milk, but many cats have a low tolerance for both of these foods.

While foods that are as much as 40 percent carbohydrate are ''well utilized'' by cats, according to the National Research Council report,[4] most veterinarians recommend that no more than a third (33 percent) of a cat's daily diet consist of carbohydrates. Otherwise, your cat may be deprived of other important nutrients. If the diet you give your cat is more than one-third carbohydrate, you should supplement with a high-protein food and some fat. Remember that although vegetables contain some proteins, the quality of these proteins (amino-acid content) isn't high enough to provide a complete feline diet.

FAT

Fat is another extremely important element in cats' daily diets. Their fat requirement is quite a bit higher than that of dogs. Not only does fat provide energy and contribute to a healthy skin and coat, it also carries the fat-soluble vitamins (A, D, E, K) throughout a cat's body. A lack of sufficient fat in a cat's diet can even make her cranky. In addition, there are fatty acids (linoleic, linolenic, and arachidonic) that cats need daily.

Many commercial diets contain added linoleic acid; dry cat foods are often sprayed with fat in order to increase their taste appeal as well as for nutritional reasons, but it may not be enough to meet a cat's optimum daily fat needs.

In order to provide the correct fat balance, your cat's daily diet should be 15 to 25 percent fat, either entirely obtained from prepared food, or added in the form of bacon drippings, butter, and vegetable cooking oils. (Don't use cod-liver oil, for too much can retard the absorption of vitamin E.) The more energetic your cat, the higher her fat requirements.

You should know, though, that fat contains more than twice as many calories per unit as either proteins or carbohydrates do, so that changes in the amount of fat you feed will greatly alter the total caloric intake of your cat. This means that you should also increase the proportion of proteins, vitamins, and minerals in order to retain nutritional balance.

Some cats will develop diarrhea if fat is added to

their diets too rapidly. Experiments show that it's best to add supplementary fat to a cat's diet gradually.[5]

MINERALS

Cats, like all animals, need some minerals in their daily diets; no specific minimum daily requirements, however, have been established yet. Minerals known to be required are: calcium, phosphorus, sodium, potassium, magnesium, iron, copper, zinc, and iodine, while others are "assumed essential by analogy with other species."[6]

Most of these minerals will automatically be provided by a varied, well-balanced diet, but may not be present in diets that are not. For instance, a cat fed a diet of nothing but unsupplemented meat will probably develop an improper calcium-to-phosphorus ratio, resulting in bone disorders. If you should happen to feed your cat nothing but canned meat (not recommended by any means), be sure that it is supplemented by calcium and phosphorus in a ratio of approximately one to one (usually slightly more calcium than phosphorus), and by vitamin D.

If you suspect that your cat has a calcium or phosphorus deficiency, don't try to remedy it by yourself, since the proportions must be exact, and some vitamin D is needed for proper absorption. Consult with your veterinarian and don't add any mineral supplements to your cat's diet indiscriminately.

Sodium chloride (ordinary table salt) is usually found in commercial cat diets. If you cook for your cat at home, a small amount of salt should be added to her food. Too much salt can lead to fluid retention and/or refusal to eat, but some should be added to a cat's diet if you want her to drink more water for any reason. It's been suggested that adding salt to a cat's diet should be instrumental in preventing the formation of urinary obstructions, but some recent experiments demonstrated that adding sodium chloride "did not prevent dietary induced calculi in male cats."[7]

The high ash (mostly mineral residue) content of many commercial cat foods has been suspect in the formation of urinary obstructions for some time. Many experiments have been done to determine the cause of these obstructions; most experts now agree that they're probably caused by a combination of several things. Dr. Patricia Scott and others have found that an excess of magnesium in the diet may be one cause of urinary problems for male cats. She concludes that "dietary magnesium levels should be kept as low as possible" and points out that the high fishbone content of some dry cat foods may contribute to high magnesium levels.[8] Ever since studies such as the one in *Consumer Reports* in 1972 publicly implicated ash as a possible contributing factor in the formation of feline urinary obstructions, most pet-food manufacturers have drastically reduced the ash content of their products. Of course, if a food contains no ash at all, it doesn't include the necessary minerals. But, in order to be on the safe side, you should look for foods that contain relatively low ash and magnesium levels if you have a male cat.

VITAMINS

Although there are limited data on the vitamin requirements of cats, researchers do know that the need for certain vitamins is quite high. Many of the required vitamins are destroyed by the high temperatures used in commercial food processing, and must be added afterward (by the manufacturer). Equally important, there are some vitamins that are toxic to cats if they're taken to excess.

As with minerals, you can usually assume that a well-balanced diet will contain all of the important vitamins your cat needs each day. Vitamin supplements should be specifically designed for cats, and ought not to be given except under a veterinarian's supervision.

The fat-soluble vitamins:

Vitamin A

Cats have a relatively high vitamin A requirement. A deficiency can cause scaly skin, loss of hair, and eye problems. On the other hand, too much vitamin A is extremely dangerous for cats and can result in severe bone disease. Thus, while liver is a very good source of vitamin A, it should be fed only occasionally (an ounce per week for a grown cat). Milk and milk products are also good sources of vitamin A. Most commercial cat foods have the correct proportion of vitamin A added to them. (Dog foods, on the other hand, don't contain enough A to meet cats' needs.)

Vitamin D

Cats' vitamin D requirements are very low. However, since this vitamin is needed in order to utilize calcium and phosphorus, it is especially important that kittens receive the correct amount. The wrong proportion of these three elements can result in uneven absorption and utilization, so that too much vitamin D can be just as harmful as too little. Indiscriminate vitamin D supplementation should be avoided.

Again, a well-balanced diet designed for cats will provide adequate D, calcium, and phosphorus. However, an unsupplemented all-meat diet will distort the balance of these three requirements, resulting in poor bone formation.

Vitamin E

While cats' vitamin E requirements are quite low, and can usually be met by a well-balanced diet, a deficiency of this vitamin can be very harmful and painful. The deficiency disease is known as steatitis, or yellow-fat disease, and is characterized by fever, lack of appetite, and pain, brought about by inflammation of body fat, so that every touch hurts. It's caused by feeding a cat too much fish oil or fish, especially red-meat tuna, with no supplementary vitamin E. And, since E is quite easily destroyed or inactivated when added to prepared foods, you shouldn't assume that you can feed an all-fish diet with impunity, even though it's been fortified with E.

Vitamin K

Cats manufacture vitamin K in their own bodies, so it doesn't need to be added to their diets. In the case of prolonged illness or the use of some medications, however, the normal balance of a cat's body may be upset and some supplementation may be necessary, but only under a doctor's supervision.

The water-soluble vitamins:

Vitamin B_1: Thiamine*

Cats' thiamine requirements are about twice that of dogs. Signs of thiamine deficiency in cats are: neuro-

---

*The B-complex vitamins, including niacin, pantothenic acid, biotin, folic acid, and sometimes choline, are often lumped together.

logical disorders, anorexia, and convulsions. Some kinds of fish (carp and saltwater herring, for instance), contain thiaminase, an enzyme that can produce a thiamine deficiency in cats.[9] Since thiamine is also easily destroyed in food processing, be sure that it is added to the diet you feed your cat.

'itamin B_2: Riboflavin

Although cats' riboflavin needs are about the same as their thiamine requirements, they are probably able to manufacture some of this substance in their own bodies when they're fed sufficient carbohydrates. Therefore, deficiency is rare when cats are fed a well-balanced diet. It is inactivated when exposed to light.[10]

Vitamin B_6: Pyridoxine

Cats' vitamin B_6 requirements are fairly low, but this is one of the vitamins that may be rendered inactive by food processing. Deficiency of the vitamin can cause weight loss, convulsions, and kidney disease. It's important, therefore, that cats' diets be supplemented with B_6.[11]

Nicotinic Acid: Niacin

While many animals can manufacture niacin in their own bodies, cats cannot. A lack of this important element leads to weakness, weight loss, and mouth disorders, including increased susceptibility to herpes. Cats lacking sufficient niacin are also very susceptible to respiratory disease.

Biotin

Biotin is required in very small amounts and is manufactured in a cat's own body. Too many raw egg whites, however, can prevent the absorption of biotin in cats' intestines. Biotin normally does not need to be added to a cat's diet.

Choline

Until recently, no minimum choline requirements had been established for cats. Choline is important in metabolizing fat and reducing cholesterol levels. Since cats consume a great deal of fat, their choline needs are fairly high.

Vitamin C: Ascorbic Acid

Although cats are able to manufacture and absorb vitamin C in their own bodies most of the time, certain kinds of illness may prevent this natural process. Many cat-food manufacturers use some ascorbic acid in the processing of their foods. Since it is "washed out" of a cat's body daily, this need be of no concern.

WATER

Many people still have the mistaken impression that cats require very little, or no, drinking water. This may stem from an unusual ability that cats share with gerbils and other desert mammals to concentrate their urine, conserving body moisture so that they can survive without much drinking water when necessary.

Under ordinary circumstances, however, depriving a cat of drinking water can be very harmful. A cat, like any other animal, can survive a loss of up to 40 percent of its body weight, but will die with only a 20 percent loss of body water.[12] Among its essential actions, water flushes out the body, removing mineral deposits and other waste materials that could otherwise cause serious problems.

The water lost from a cat's body each day through waste, respiration, and evaporation must be replaced. To do this, the average grown cat needs about a cup and a quarter (one ounce per pound) of water daily. Special circumstances, such as extreme heat, unusually vigorous exercise, fever, diarrhea, and other illnesses, can lead to a more-than-average moisture loss, and dehydrate a cat.

Some of your cat's daily water requirement may be filled by the moisture in her food, but it's foolish to worry about exactly how much more to give her. Providing plenty of fresh, clean water at all times will allow your pet to drink the amount she needs, when she needs it. If for some reason you can't leave a bowl of water around all the time, offer water to your cat at least three times a day.

Cats are usually very fussy about the water they drink. Our two cats won't drink from a bowl that a dog with a dirty muzzle has just slurped from but will wait none too patiently while I rinse the bowl out and fill it with fresh water. Some cats also like to sip from a dripping faucet or freshly flushed toilet bowl (be careful of cleaning agents if your cat does this). Francis, for instance, thought that we provided a dripping faucet just for him, and was annoyed when we finally had it fixed. Still other cats, apparently defying the clean-water theory, drink any water they can locate, from plant saucers to pots soaking in the sink—perhaps something in the water tastes good. This habit of drinking standing water should be discouraged by providing plenty of fresh water, perhaps bowls in several rooms if your house is large. It could get your cat in bad trouble if, for instance, she drinks from a puddle or jar containing something poisonous.

Occasionally, a cat won't seem to know enough to drink sufficient water. For instance, a cat who's been eating very moist food and is suddenly switched to a drier diet may not be in the habit of drinking much water. If coaxing doesn't work, try adding a few grains of salt to her food for a few days. This may make her thirsty enough to start drinking water. If milk agrees with your cat, this can also provide needed moisture.

If your cat suddenly starts to drink excessive amounts of water while her diet remains the same, it can be a sign of fever, urinary problems, or other illness. Consult your veterinarian if the unusual drinking goes on for more than a few days.

How Much to Feed Your Cat

The average grown cat needs anywhere from 25 to 40 calories per pound of body weight each day. The need is approximate because there are so many variations in activity level, climate, and physical changes created by pregnancy, illness, and so forth. Age, of course, also alters caloric requirements. Kittens need much more food energy, or calories, per pound of body weight than adult cats, in order to grow and develop. When they're ten weeks old, kittens need about 113 calories per pound of weight each day. Their need decreases rapidly to only about 50 calories per pound when they're six months old, and so on in a less precipitous decline until adulthood. Table 1 can serve as a general guideline to calorie needs, but before you start to count your pet's calories, remember that healthy cats are very good at regulating their own food intake as needed, provided that they're given the chance and are fed a nutritionally balanced diet.

How much food you actually give a cat to meet her caloric and nutritional requirements depends in part on what kind of food, or foods, you feed her. A glance at Table 2 will show you how much the three major types of commercial cat foods vary in caloric content. For example, you have to feed almost three times as much "moist," or canned, food as dry, in order to give your cat the same number of calories. The three kinds of food also differ in other ways. Although different brands of commercial cat food may vary as to actual ingredients, each particular kind (dry, semi-moist, canned) has some general characteristics.

Choosing Foods

COMMERCIAL VS. "HOME-COOKED" FOOD

Although you can provide a completely nutritious diet for your cat with fresh, home-prepared foods, it's not easy. If you're determined to try, you'll need to learn a great deal about feline nutrition and be prepared to measure and weigh the various components of the food you serve if you want to achieve the proper balance. If you feed your cat nothing but home-cooked foods, you'll also need to add a vitamin-mineral supplement daily to be sure that your pet is receiving all the necessary nutrients. Be sure to get a preparation designed only for cats (from a veterinarian, ideally), and follow directions carefully.

Not only is all this time-consuming, but it can end up being a good deal more costly than serving commercially prepared foods on a regular basis. This doesn't mean that you can't cook up an occasional treat for your pet, if you enjoy doing it, but for regular daily use, well-chosen commercial cat foods are by far the most satisfactory, convenient, and nutritionally complete.

Choosing the best commercial foods for your cat can be something of a trial. Commercials, printed advertisements, fancy boxes, and the flood of "new" and "improved" products on the market can be extremely confusing. While you don't necessarily have to buy the most expensive product on the shelf, bear in mind that the major pet-food companies are extremely conscientious about their products, and maintain up-to-date research and testing laboratories. You should really be choosing the food your cat is going to eat on the basis of consistent and controlled quality. Remember that "eye appeal" is for you, the buyer, and not for your pet. Fancy packaging or cute shapes don't mean a thing to a cat, or to her nutritional balance, while they do add to the cost. Use your own good judgment in this respect.

Learn to read labels. If the food provides "100 percent nutrition" or is "a complete diet," the label will say so. If there is no such statement, or the label says that the food is merely "balanced," or is a "supplement" or "treat," then it shouldn't be fed exclusively. Look in the contents list for added vitamins and minerals, many of which are destroyed in preparation. Be aware that listings such as "crude protein content" don't mean that your cat will be able to use all of that protein.

The next step is to try various selected foods out on your cat. Give only small quantities of each new food until you can determine whether it agrees with your pet. Naturally, if a particular food gives your pet diarrhea or excessive gas, for instance, discontinue it. You or your cat may not like the appearance or aroma of some foods. Only by trying out a number of foods can you find out what suits your pet best, but don't be conned into sticking to only one kind or flavor. Accustom your pet to variety early in life.

The best kind of diet for cats is a varied one. Cats should be taught to eat not only many flavors, but various types of food. I always feed my cats some of each kind: some dry food left out for snacking; some semi-moist food as a before-bedtime treat; and some moist, canned food once a day, for "dinner." Whatever combination you choose, it will make your life much easier if you accustom your cat to eating food in more than one form. Not only will variety provide good nutrition, it will ensure that the cat won't go hungry if she has to board or travel at any time in her life, or needs to have a special diet for any reason.

Table 1 *Approximate Recommended Daily Calorie Allowances for Cats**

KITTEN	Calories per pound of body weight
10 weeks	113
20 weeks	58.96
30 weeks	45
40 weeks	36
ADULT 50 weeks and over	Calories per pound of body weight
Inactive	31.7
Active	36.28
Gestating	45.36
Lactating—6th week	103.4 (4 kittens)
	145 (6 kittens)

*Assuming a 4, 4, 9 caloric ratio of protein, carbohydrate, fat.

ADAPTED FROM *Nutrient Requirements of Cats*, © 1986, by the National Academy Press, National Academy of Sciences, Washington, DC.

DRY FOOD

Dry food is very low in moisture. It is about 90 percent solid, or dry, material, so it's especially important that you provide plenty of drinking water to offset this lack, even if only part of your cat's diet consists of dry food.

Dry cat foods usually are a combination of many ingredients and supplements and provide a very good base for your cat's diet. As you can see from Table 2, dry food is high in calories—almost three times as high per portion as canned foods. Munching dry food is also very good for cats' teeth and gums. It is less expensive, per portion, than either semimoist or canned cat food.

Dry cat foods do have some drawbacks, however. As I pointed out under "minerals," the high ash and magnesium levels in some dry cat foods make them risky as an exclusive diet. In addition, although most dry cat foods are now sprayed with fats and oils to add to palatability and nutrition, it is usually not enough to meet a cat's optimum daily fat needs. If you feed your cat a great deal of dry food that is less than 15 percent fat, you should supplement with a scant tablespoon of fat (butter, vegetable oil, bacon drippings) for each four-ounce serving of dry food fed.

Small kittens shouldn't be fed dry food at all, unless it's softened with broth or water, until they learn to chew well.

SEMIMOIST FOOD

Semimoist cat foods contain about three times as much water as dry cat foods do. They are generally made up of a well-balanced mixture of a number of ingredients, just as dry foods are, and they supply good nutrition. The exception, again, is usually insufficient fat, which must be added if this kind of food is used exclusively, up to the recommended dietary level. Their soft consistency makes them more palatable than dry food for some cats.

Unfortunately, the ingredients that keep these foods soft and moist (sugar, sorbates, etc.)[13] disagree with some cats and give them diarrhea when too much semimoist food is eaten. In addition, semimoist foods provide very little exercise for your cat's teeth and jaws.

Semimoist cat foods are excellent as treats to feed your cat if she likes them. They usually come in serving-size pouches, and are expensive compared with dry foods.

CANNED FOODS

Canned cat foods contain a lot of moisture, with as little as 25 percent solid matter in some. They're usually made up of one main ingredient, such as meat, poultry, or fish, mixed with grains or cereals and supplemented with minerals and vitamins. Most cats love them and will eat them eagerly.

It's especially important to read the labels on canned cat foods carefully, because many of them are not designed to provide complete nutrition, but are to be fed only as supplements. The protein and fat content of canned cat foods is generally very good, but other important ingredients may be missing. If you feed them along with either some dry or semimoist foods daily, this needn't worry you.

Canned cat foods are much lower in caloric value, per portion, than either dry or semimoist foods (see Table 2), so a great deal more must be fed in order to meet your cat's needs. They are also a lot more expensive, per serving, than either of the other two types of food.

Table 2 *Approximate Daily Food Allowances of Cats Using Dry, Semimoist, and Canned Cat Foods*

Cat	Approximate average weight (lbs.)	Type of Food		
		Dry Type[a]	Semimoist Type[b]	Canned Type[c]
		(average ounces/cat)		
KITTEN				
10 weeks	2.2	2.7	2.9	7.99
20 weeks	3.8	3.17	3.3	9.00
30 weeks	6.9	3.45	3.65	10
40 weeks	7.4	2.96	3.17	8.6
ADULT 50 weeks and over				
Inactive	7.2	2.4	2.6	7.48
Active	7.2	2.96	3.19	8.6
Gestating	7.2	3.56	3.78	10.4
Lactating	7.2	8.5	9	24.8

a Dry matter, 90%
b Dry matter, 70%
c Dry matter, 25%
d Queens nursing 4–5 kittens in 6th week of lactation.

ADAPTED FROM *Nutrient Requirements of Cats*, © 1986, by the National Academy Press, National Academy of Sciences, Washington, DC.

SPECIAL DIETS

Sometimes special canned cat foods, available through veterinarians, are used as a matter of course by breeders and owners because of their excellent balance of nutrients and the ease with which cats can utilize them. These special diets are expensive and are usually not necessary, unless your cat has been raised on them, or your doctor recommends them.

On the other hand, there are now prescription diets available for cats, which are designed to meet certain specific medical conditions, such as diabetes, overweight, urinary problems, and so forth. Dispensed by veterinarians, these scientifically prepared foods can do a great deal to prolong the life of a cat who would have little chance for survival otherwise.

The fact that your cat may someday have to eat one of these special diets is just one more reason to accustom her to accepting a variety of foods early in life.

TREATS

While a well-balanced combination of commercial cat foods will certainly maintain your cat nutritionally, you may enjoy adding something extra from time to time. Your cat will appreciate an occasional treat, and you'll have fun watching her relish it. It's all right to let your cat eat small amounts of almost any kind of people-food that she likes. I've known cats who liked such bizarre things as sesame-seed crackers and grapes. Just be sure not to let your cat overindulge until you know how her insides will react. Exceptions are: highly seasoned foods, raw meat or fish; bones that either can be swallowed or can splinter; anything that isn't fresh.

Bones large enough not to swallow and hard enough not to splinter when chewed can provide beneficial jaw exercise. They should be boiled or roasted first, to destroy harmful parasites.

Eggs are very good for cats. Remember, though, that too much uncooked egg white destroys biotin, so either give only the yolk, or cook eggs lightly before serving.

Flavorings, such as garlic and onion powder or juice, and leftover soups or gravies, make foods taste better.

Fresh fish is an all-time cat favorite. Cook the fish lightly to destroy parasites, and cut it into easily handled pieces.

Fresh meats and poultry, again cooked lightly, are also a great treat for cats. Cut the cooked meat into chunks that your pet can handle easily.

Most cats also like *fresh vegetables*. Raw vegetables seem to give most cats diarrhea, so cook them lightly and offer either alone, or chopped up and mixed with other foods.

Cats also love to nibble on fresh *greens*, such as grasses or catnip. You can grow your pet's own supply of these treats, indoors or out, and either let your pet chew on them as they grow, or cut them off and offer them on a plate. If you grow greens indoors in a pot, be sure to keep them in a completely different spot than you do any houseplants, so that there's no confusion on your cat's part as to which plants are hers.

Many cats love *milk*, but it gives some diarrhea. If your cat can't drink milk, try giving her a little *cottage cheese* or *yogurt*, since many cats can digest these products better than plain milk. Other kinds of *cheese* are also often cat favorites.

Organ meats, especially beef liver, are real treats for cats. Liver, which is the richest in nutrients, can cause problems if too much is given, so limit your cat's liver intake to about an ounce a week. Be sure to cook all organ meats lightly. Leftovers can be stored in the freezer for some time.

If you want to go a step further than simply offering a single treat to your cat, and cook her a whole meal now and then, there are two excellent pet cookbooks: *The Healthy Cat & Dog Cook Book*, by Joan Harper, and *Dr. Terri McGinnis' Dog & Cat Good Food Book*.

Remember that these foods should be served as treats. Don't let your cat get so used to eating these special foods that she neglects her regular diet, or else her nutritional balance will be thrown off.

Feeding Problems

> What cat's averse to fish?
> —THOMAS GRAY,
> "On the Death of a Favorite Cat"

It's all very well to know about cats' nutritional requirements, but what do you do if your cat simply won't eat right or won't eat enough, for one reason or another? How do you get a finicky cat to try new foods, or a noneater to eat like a cat instead of a bird?

Contrary to popular belief, finicky cats aren't born. They're created. According to the panelists at the National Research Council, "cats . . . frequently exhibit food preferences that have been conditioned by previous dietary experiences. Conditioned diet preferences should not be confused with nutrient requirements."[14]

The most common "conditioned diet preference" for cats is fish. An exclusive diet of fish, or any other food, is detrimental from a nutritional standpoint; an extreme food phobia, or finickiness, can create other serious problems, too. Pong, an altered Siamese who lived with us for about seven years when I was growing up, was fed nothing but cooked codfish fillets from the time he was weaned. We were told that that was all he'd eat by the lady who bred him and we never taught him to eat anything else. My mother always sprinkled a vitamin-mineral powder supplied by the veterinarian on Pong's meals, and he seemed healthy. One summer, however, we left him in someone else's care for a month. All was fine until his sitter had a family emergency and had to put him in a boarding kennel, where they didn't prepare cod fillets for him. By the time we returned, he was almost dead from starvation and dehydration, and despite forced feeding and lots of TLC, he never fully recovered and died shortly afterward. Although the separation from his family probably had something to do with it, he had been left with a sitter before and fared well. I'm sure that he would have survived if he just hadn't been so finicky and had been able to eat something.

RETRAINING A FINICKY CAT

A finicky cat can be reconditioned to accept a variety of foods. In the past, experts used to advocate starving a cat for several days in order to force her to eat what you offered. I think that this is unnecessarily hard on both of you, and I can't imagine having a hungry, screaming cat around for very long. It's far easier to trick your cat into accepting new foods, one at a time.

To introduce a new food, or type of food, to a finicky cat, you'll have to go about it gradually. You can use cats' strong smell conditioning to your advantage. If your cat is a fish lover, for instance, the smell of the fish will mask the odor of other foods. Start by mixing a very small amount of the new food with your cat's usual fish dish for a few days. If she's at all suspicious, reduce the amount of new food. Once she's accepting the mixture happily, increase the percentage of new food slightly, and so on, until she'll eat a fairly large portion of the new food alone. A little gravy made up of warm water and a bit of fish flavor may help her to enjoy the new food more.

Cats also love garlic and onion, and mixing some powder or juice with a new food may induce a fussy cat to try it. Adding a bit of meat or poultry gravy, or some milk if your cat can tolerate it, is a good way to start a cat off on dry food. You'll want to reduce the liquid gradually, however, until she'll eat the food completely dry in order to benefit from the chewing action.

OTHER FEEDING PROBLEMS

In addition to food preferences, cats sometimes develop rigid feeding routines. While owners are usually willing to go along with these routines, it's foolish to let a cat become too dependent on them. Don't let only one family member feed a cat, for instance, or your pet may not eat if that person is away.

If you have a cat who doesn't eat well at all, no matter what you feed her, there can be several reasons. First, of course, is a physical problem. If your cat seems to have no interest in food or has trouble chewing or swallowing, she should see a doctor right away. She could be sick, or have some kind of blockage or a mouth or breathing problem that is preventing her from eating.

A highly strung cat may not eat if there's too much noise or confusion in the room. Running, shouting, or even loud voices can make some cats so nervous that they can't eat. Other kinds of stress, such as the absence of a loved one, the presence of a new pet, a move, or a sudden drastic change in household routine, can also make a cat too nervous and upset to eat.

Other pets can make mealtime stressful, especially for a nonaggressive cat. Faced with a competitor for her food, a cat may either bolt her food so fast that she immediately throws it right back up, or give up completely and walk away.

The cleanliness and condition of feeding dishes may

have a surprising effect on cats, even on those who are usually quite adaptable. In her report on cats' nutritional needs, Dr. Patricia Scott tells of a situation in which a ". . . change in the type of disinfectant used to wash the dishes" caused a group of laboratory cats to lose ". . . a great deal of weight during the course of one week."[15]

Food that's icy cold will be rejected by many cats. Feed canned or fresh foods at room temperature, or warm them with hot water or gravy before serving.

Finally, the consistency, taste, or aroma of the food or foods you're offering may not appeal to your cat. Perhaps the brand you're using may not be right for your pet's particular tastes, even though it's a perfectly good food that other cats will accept.

By understanding and anticipating some of the things that can turn a healthy cat into a problem eater, you'll be able to avoid creating a finicky cat. If you know that your pet is upset by noise, for instance, you'll allow her to eat in peace and quiet. If she's disturbed by another cat, give her her own plate. A little thoughtfulness on your part from the start can prevent serious eating problems from developing.

A Word to the Wise

Recently, onion poisoning has been described in cats. And, although it has not yet been reported in cats, cocoa and related products have been proved to be toxic to dogs. So, the National Academy of Sciences recommends avoiding these foods because of their possible adverse effects.[16]

Excesses to Avoid

> More ways of killing a cat than choking
> her with cream.
> —CHARLES KINGSLEY, *Westward Ho*

On the other end of the spectrum is the cat who either eats too much altogether, or whose owner feeds her too much of certain foods.

Although most cats won't overeat, sometimes it's very hard for a pet to resist her owner's urgings and plyings. A cat who is offered a constant parade of overrich foods will end up fat. So will a cat whose owner frequently hand-feeds her from his own plate, giving her too much high-calorie people-food. Letting your cat become overweight is doing her no favor. It will reduce her life expectancy and put undue strain on her entire body. A fat cat can no longer run and jump and play, and loses all of her energy and vitality.

If you suspect that your cat is overweight, take her to the doctor, who may suggest a special diet, or tell you just how much to cut back on your cat's regular daily food intake. Weigh your cat daily until she reaches the desired weight. Then keep her slim on a good maintenance diet, following the calorie allowance in Table 1.

Other dietary excesses don't have such visible results as simple overfeeding, but they can be just as harmful. The following chart summarizes some of the most common ones.

A Summary of Excesses to Avoid in Cats' Diets*

Food	Results
Too much fish or fish oil, especially tuna (no vitamin E supplementation)	Vitamin E lack, resulting in steatitis (yellow-fat disease), characterized by inflammation of fat tissues, pain, fever, and loss of appetite
Too much raw liver and milk (near-exclusive diet)	Vitamin A toxicity, characterized by dark diarrhea, leading to a number of irregularities, particularly skeletal
Too much muscle or organ meat (improper supplementation)	Upset of calcium-phosphorus balance, resulting in poor bone formation and locomotor problems
Too much cooked horsemeat (exclusive diet)[17]	Folic acid lack, causing poor growth and anemia
Too much of some kinds of raw or canned fish containing thiaminase (carp, saltwater herring)	Thiamine deficiency, resulting in neurological disorders, seizures, anorexia, weakness, and eventual death
Too much raw egg white	No biotin absorption in intestines, resulting in secretions around eyes, nose, and mouth; dermatitis; and emaciation
Too much ash (mineral residue)	Possible factor contributing to urinary obstructions
Too much magnesium[18]	Possible factor contributing to urinary obstructions
Too much salt[19]	Excessive fluid retention, puffiness. In cases of heart disease, other possibly detrimental effects
Too much cow's milk	Diarrhea, flatulence

*Based on *Nutrient Requirements of Cats*, except where otherwise noted.

Notes—Chapter 4

1. ". . . the requirement of the adult cat (for protein) is nearly *five* times that of the adult dog." James G. Morris, Ph.D., and Quinton R. Rogers, Ph.D., "The Cat's High Protein Requirement," *Friskies Research Digest*, Vol. 14, No. 2, Summer 1978 (Friskies Pet Foods Division of Carnation Co., Pico Rivera, California).

2. *Nutrient Requirements of Cats*, © 1986, National Academy Press, National Academy of Sciences, Washington, D.C., pp. 13–15.

3. Morris, J.J., Rogers, Q.R., and Pion, P.D., International Symposium: Nutrition, Malnutrition and Diet of Cats and Dogs. Hannover, West Germany, August, 1987. (Abstr.)

4. National Academy of Sciences, p. 6.

5. Dr. Patricia P. Scott, "The Nutritional Requirements of Cats," *Basic Guide to Canine Nutrition*, Gaines Professional Services, White Plains, NY, 1977.

6. National Academy of Sciences, p. 15.

7. Dwayne Jamar, Ph.D., F.C.H. Chow, Ph.D., M.I. Dysart, B.S., L.J. Rich, DVM, Ph.D, "Effect of Sodium Chloride in Prevention of Experimentally Produced Phosphate Uroliths in Male Cats," *The Journal of American Animal Hospital Association*, Vol. 12, No. 4, July/August 1976.

8. Scott, p. 89.

9. Ibid., p. 86, and National Academy of Sciences, p. 24.

10. National Academy of Sciences, p. 25.

11. Ibid., p. 26.

12. Ibid., p. 29.

13. Ibid., p. 30.

14. Ibid., p. 30.

15. Scott, p. 92.

16. National Academy of Sciences, pp. 35–36.

17. Scott, p. 87.

18. Ibid., p. 89.

19. Olive Evans, "Many Pet Foods, Too, Are High in Salt Content," based on an interview with Dr. Robert L. Hamlin of Ohio State University, *The New York Times*, August 11, 1979.

5

A Healthy Cat Is a Happy Cat

It has been the providence of Nature to
give this creature nine lives instead of one.
—PILPAY,
"The Greedy and Ambitious Cat,"
Fable III

The notion expressed by Pilpay around the fourth century B.C. persists even today. There are people who believe that a cat is practically indestructible and needs no particular health care to survive. Just recently, when I mentioned to someone that I was going to take Wilbur to the doctor for his yearly booster shots, I was greeted with an amazed stare. "Cats need shots?" asked the person I was talking to. When I answered "Yes," the man regaled me with stories of numerous cats he'd owned as a boy, who'd "done very well" without such nonsense!

It is true that cats have an uncanny ability to get along without much help, but only for a relatively short time. Friends adopted a beat-up tomcat who started coming to their door for handouts during a particularly severe winter a few years ago. When they'd gained his trust sufficiently, they took him to the veterinarian to be checked over. They weren't going to bother having him neutered, because he seemed very old: not only was he scarred and battered, but he moved slowly and stiffly like an old man. Much to their amazement, the doctor estimated his age at only about five years at the most. Despite their best efforts, Tom lived only for about six more months—his hard life had taken its toll.

There have been a lot of changes in our knowledge about cat care since my skeptical friend had cats as a boy. A great deal has been learned in the past three or four decades about how to protect cats against infectious illnesses and cure them when they're unwell. If you're going to invest time and affection on a pet cat, you'll surely want to do all that you can to keep her healthy and free from pain and discomfort, and ensure the longest possible life expectancy. You can't always protect your cat against every illness, but there are certain things you can do to help keep her well. The first and most important step is to choose a veterinarian whom you can trust and your cat can tolerate. Then, following your doctor's advice as to exact dosage and timing, have your pet immunized against the most common and infectious cat diseases.

It's also important to be aware of some common cat complaints and signs of illness. I remember well when a lovely, fat cat named Conrad, who belonged to a little girl we knew, died of uremic poisoning because his owners had no idea that cats could develop urinary stoppages. They didn't recognize his symptoms and get help until he was in bad trouble, and by then it was too late for the doctor to save him.

I'm not going to attempt to include in this chapter all of the ailments a cat can possibly get—there are far too many, most of which can be diagnosed only by a professional. But you should be able to spot some general signs of trouble so that you can have your pet treated for a disorder before it becomes serious.

Keeping Your Cat Well

CHOOSING THE RIGHT DOCTOR

Step one in preventive care, as I said before, is finding a good veterinarian who'll work out well for you and your cat. Depending on where you live, you may have a number of animal doctors to choose from, and it's important to select one whom you trust, understand, and can stay with throughout your pet's lifetime. A doctor can really tell just how well your cat is doing at a given time only if he's seen her on a regular basis.

The best source of information about veterinarians is usually other intelligent cat owners or breeders. Not all veterinarians especially like handling cats, so be sure to choose one whose practice includes a large percentage of cats. You can tell a great deal about how a veterinarian feels toward cats by observing how he handles your pet on the first visit, and how interested he is in her. This is more important than you may think. I don't believe that it's going too far to say that most cats seem to sense immediately when people don't like them, and it will only make all visits to the doctor that much harder if your cat instinctively distrusts her veterinarian.

Look around the office on your first visit. If the doctor is unknown to you, you should check his credentials, and note any national, state, or local professional organizations that he belongs to. These documents are usually prominently displayed somewhere—if you see none, ask. While fancy decorations don't indicate much about a doctor's competence, other external things do make a difference. Many animal illnesses are highly contagious, so examining rooms should be spotlessly clean, and the tables sterilized after each

111

patient. Ask to visit the area where patients stay when they have to be kept overnight, or for part of a day; these areas should also be clean and free from offensive odors. Most doctors are happy to show you around at a convenient time; if yours is reluctant to do so, you should wonder why.

Find out if the doctor is willing to answer questions over the telephone, and when his scheduled calling hours are. You should also ask what arrangements he makes for covering his practice in cases of emergency when he's off duty. Be sure, too, that you're able to understand him; that he doesn't talk over your head, or in a confusing way; and that he's willing to discuss all aspects of your cat's care with you.

If the first doctor you visit doesn't come up to your standards of cleanliness, or makes you uncomfortable or nervous, or acts as if you're inconveniencing him with your questions, find another veterinarian. Your pet's good health, and your own peace of mind, are dependent on having a reliable, interested, up-to-date doctor, and you shouldn't settle for anything less.

A successful relationship with a veterinarian isn't a one-way street, however, and there are certain things you should remember in your dealings with a busy professional. If the doctor or his staff are constantly irritated at *you*, because of thoughtless behavior, it may be hard for them to treat your pet with patience. When you make an appointment, it's a good idea to say just what it is you're coming in for, so that the proper amount of time can be allotted: a booster shot takes less than ten minutes, while a complete examination can last much longer. (Most veterinarians, by the way, use a booster-shot visit as occasion for a checkup.) Be on time. Even if you have to wait a few minutes because of an emergency or other schedule upset, don't keep the doctor waiting for you. Expect to stay and help with your pet unless you've been told that you'll be leaving her for treatment—your veterinarian's office isn't a drop-off animal-care center. Don't ask for unusual, time-consuming services or treatments when the office is crowded if you haven't made arrangements in advance.

Calling can often take the place of an office visit, but don't call during nonoffice hours for advice on routine matters. On the other hand, don't wait to call or visit the doctor until an emergency situation has developed. Last, but certainly not least, pay your veterinarian bills promptly. (Many animal doctors now ask to be paid on the spot.) Your doctor has many expenses in running an up-to-date office with an efficient staff, and shouldn't have to wait for his money. If you can pay only a little at a time, make arrangements in advance.

A CARRYING CASE

Before discussing what to expect on your first veterinary visit, I want to remind you about one of the most important pieces of cat equipment that you can have—a sturdy, roomy, cat carrying case. Not only do most veterinarians insist that their feline patients arrive in a carrier, it's really the only safe way to transport any cat. No matter how calm and brave your cat may be, arriving in a strange waiting room that may be populated with unknown animals as well as people is likely to send her into a panic. The results can be painful, as she digs her claws into your shoulders and arms. It can also be dangerous for your pet if she manages to escape. Nothing will start your first visit to the doctor off on a worse note than a frantic, hysterical game of "catch the cat."

If your cat is very young, and you haven't had a

113

chance to purchase a carrying case yet, a strong card-board carton, with appropriate air holes and an escape-proof closing, will do in a pinch. Be very careful, though, because even the frailest-seeming kitten gains supercat strength when frightened, and can become an amazingly good escape artist. *Don't* rely on a carton to transport your pet in if you're driving by yourself.

Two kitten-in-car incidents come to mind. A friend's son once did about nine hundred dollars' worth of damage to a brand-new station wagon when a tiny eight-week-old kitten unexpectedly dug her claws into his ankle. The kitten was on her way to the pound, but after that the family decided that they'd better keep her because she'd cost them so much money! On the other occasion my husband was taking Oliver, a three-month-old black-and-white kitten, to the veterinarian. For some reason we had no carrier at the time, and had put Oliver in a carton with the top taped closed. As my husband reached a busy intersection, some-thing flashed by his elbow and out the open front win-dow. It took him a minute to realize that the object that had just gone out the window and disappeared into the bushes was Oliver, who'd wormed his way out of a small crack in the top of the carton. After search-ing and calling, he finally came home with no kitten. I went back with him, expecting the worst, and, as cars and trucks whizzed by, we finally located Oliver, sitting quite calmly under a low bush. This time, I sat in the car and held the lid of the carton closed, as Oliver continued to struggle to get out.

These two stories had relatively happy endings—no permanent damage was done to people or pets, but taking a cat or kitten in a car without a sturdy carrier can be very hazardous. Even the so-called temporary carrying cases breeders and pet stores sometimes pro-vide aren't much good, because the closures aren't catproof for more than a few minutes unless there's someone around to hold them shut.

I must add that there are a few rare cats who don't seem to be afraid to ride in a car. Peter, for instance, used to lie on the small shelf below the rear window of our car when we went away for the summer. He seemed to enjoy looking out and, as I mentioned before, he also liked to be admired. He had apparently been riding in cars since he was a small kitten, and was a completely unflappable animal. Since then I've occasionally seen a cat riding in the same spot, but it's very unusual for a cat to stay that calm in a car; often, even cats who ride well on local trips will be frightened by highway noise. If you have one of those cats who enjoy car travel, remember to take extreme care when you stop so that she doesn't jump out and get lost or hurt.

If you're going to have a cat as a pet, you'll be using a carrier for her entire life, so you might as well get a good one to start with. The case needn't be fancy, but it must be strong and crush-proof with good fasteners. It should also be roomy enough for a grown cat to stand or lie down in, and easy to clean or wash if necessary. The carrier must also have ample ventilation—some have cloth flaps that can snap over the air vents in case of severe cold or very scared cats, but I don't think that these flaps are usually needed.

We used to have a carrier that opened at one end, and it was a disaster. No sooner would I get a cat's rear end into it and be ready to close it than some other part of her body would be sticking out. It took at least two people to stuff the poor cat into the carrier, and by the time she was closed in, she'd be thoroughly upset and we'd be exhausted. So be sure to purchase a carrying case that opens at the top (most are made this way now). Then you can simply pop your pet in and close the lid. It's also much easier to lift a reluctant cat out of a top-opening carrier than to have to drag her out from one end. Some cases have transparent tops or wire sides, so that you can see the cat, and she can look out. I'm not sure that it's a good idea for a cat to be able to see out that well, however, since strange sights may simply upset her unless she's very used to riding in a case.

Once you've bought a good carrying case, you can help your cat become familiar with it by leaving it open on the floor. Put a towel or sweater in the bottom, and your pet probably won't be able to resist getting in—she may even go to sleep in it. While your pet may never learn to actually enjoy riding in her carrying case, especially if the only place she ever goes in it is to the doctor, if she's allowed to get used to it gradually in her own home, she'll at least feel secure in it.

YOUR CAT'S FIRST VISIT TO THE DOCTOR

Making It Less Traumatic

Your cat should get used to going to the doctor as early as possible. Ideally, your first visit to the veterinarian should be before you even take her home. Having your new cat checked out then is a good idea for several reasons: if there's anything seriously wrong with her, you'll be able to return her to the breeder before you become attached to her; if you have other pets now, or have had them in your house in the past, and your new cat hasn't been properly immunized, she can be protected before she's exposed to any new germs; your veterinarian can assist you in selecting the proper diet for your new pet and set up a schedule for shots and boosters; and, even more important, your

ABOVE:
Wilbur is waiting for a clean water bowl

Elizabeth Randolph and Wilbur

ABOVE:
Surveying the scene

*Randolph and Patrick
enjoying their "tree"*

pet will officially be the doctor's patient—her record will be on file, and the veterinarian will be able to observe her growth and development in subsequent visits. If you can't arrange a veterinary visit on your way home, make an appointment as soon as you possibly can.

No matter when your cat's first visit to the doctor's office occurs, it's apt to be a bewildering and somewhat frightening experience for her. For all their bravado in familiar territory, most cats are very wary of strange places and of being handled by people who are new to them. Your attitude can help a great deal. If you're nervous, some of your uncertainty will communicate itself to your cat. That's why it's so important to choose a doctor who likes cats and isn't at all frightened of them. Calm, sure handling will do a great deal to allay a cat's feeling of insecurity.

Most veterinarians ask owners to help them by holding a pet when she's being examined. The way to hold a cat on the examining table is to grasp her front legs firmly in one hand, from behind, while stroking and petting her head with the other hand. If your cat tries to bite while the doctor is examining her or giving her a shot, grasp the loose skin at the back of her neck with your free hand and shake her head. This will distract her and prevent her from being able to turn around and bite. Talking in a soothing way may help, but if your cat is truly frightened, she may not even hear you.

The doctor may ask you to assist him in other ways, and you should try to do anything he asks with a firm sure touch. If you're at all tentative, your pet will sense it and take advantage. There are restraints that can be used, and sometimes pets even have to be lightly anesthetized in order to be worked on, but these methods

117

are used by most doctors only in extremes, and are to be avoided if at all possible.

You should have your cat's carrier open nearby; she can be popped into it the minute the examination is over if she shows signs of terror or wildness, or tries to scratch or run off. Once she's inside the safety of her carrying case, your cat will calm down quickly.

A Physical for Your Cat—What to Expect

The first time that you and your cat visit the veterinarian, the doctor will want to begin with a health history. He'll want to know as much as possible about your pet's background, health, and immunizations up to now. He'll probably also ask about your cat's food and water consumption; bowel and bladder functions; activity level; and general health. If you've just gotten your pet, and don't know much about her background, don't worry, but answer any questions you can.

A physical for a cat is very similar to one given a human. In order to assess the patient's general health, the doctor will give her a thorough external going-over. He'll probably weigh her and take her temperature with a rectal thermometer. (Have him show you how to do this at home.) Next, he'll check the cat's eyes, ears, nose, skin and coat, mouth, teeth, gums, throat, anal and genital area, take her pulse, note her breathing, and listen to her heart with a stethoscope. In addition, he'll examine the cat's entire body with his hands, gently palpitating her stomach, feeling her legs, feet, and spine. Don't be alarmed if your pet moans or makes noises when she's being examined—she's probably expressing indignation, not pain.

If you think you notice the doctor sniffing your cat, you're not mistaken. He's using his nose to determine if there's any foul odor around her skin, mouth, or ears that might signify infection or disease.

If he thinks it's called for, the veterinarian may use further tests to evaluate your cat, such as X rays, radiographs, electrocardiograms, or some laboratory tests. If your cat has never been tested for worms, you'll probably be asked to bring in a stool sample later on for microscopic examination.

Shots

Unless further tests or examinations seem necessary to the doctor, once the exam is completed your pet will be started on her immunizations. Even if a young kitten has had her "temporary" shots, she may need more protection now, especially if there are, or ever have been, other cats in your household. We once lost a dear little Siamese kitten because we relied on the "temporary" shots the seller assured us she'd had, which apparently either had worn off or were not adequate in the first place.

Many cat diseases are highly contagious, but none more than feline distemper (panleukopenia, or enteritis). This disease is so virulent that its germs can be present in a household for as long as a year after a sick animal has been in residence, and it can be carried on human hands or clothing. Young kittens are particularly susceptible to distemper, and their recovery rate is low, so they must be protected against it right away. (This is the disease that our little Siamese succumbed to.)

There are also several very infectious, upper respiratory coldlike infections to which cats, especially young ones, are very subject. A combined vaccine, called FVRCP, protects against distemper and several of these respiratory infections at once, and many doc-

119

tors now use it. It is usually given three times in the first year of a cat's life, with yearly boosters thereafter. Depending on where you live and other factors, your veterinarian may also suggest special immunization against pneumonitis, another highly infectious respiratory disease.

Rabies shots are also essential for any cat, regardless of whether or not she usually stays indoors. A booster is required at regular intervals.

In 1984, a vaccine against FeLV (feline leukemia virus) was approved. Prior to this, FeLV, which decreases the ability of a cat's immune system to fight disease, was a leading killer of cats. After three initial vaccinations, a yearly booster should be given to adult cats.

The doctor will be aware of the presence of any other illness or diseases in your area and can advise you best how to protect your cat against them. He'll then set up a schedule for further shots and boosters, which will depend on the type of vaccine used, the age of the cat, and other variables.

If the expense or inconvenience of these immunizations bothers you, bear in mind that the diseases they protect against can be extremely difficult and costly to cure at best, and at worst (rabies, for example), incurable. Don't let yourself become complacent later on in your cat's life and assume that just because she's never been ill she doesn't need continued protection. Not only can a cat's degree of resistance to disease vary during a lifetime, but new animals and changing situations in your neighborhood can expose her to infection at any time. The very best preventive medicine for your pet is an up-to-date series of shots. The yearly visit for boosters is also an excellent opportunity for the doctor to check over your older cat.

Once your cat is safely back in her carrying case,

120

ask any questions you may have about feeding, booster shots, or other routines for your new pet. Many doctors give their patients a card or flier with printed care instructions. If your veterinarian doesn't do this, it's a good idea to jot his directions down, so you don't forget what he said the minute you get home.

SURGICAL PROCEDURES

Neutering

On your first visit to the veterinarian, you should discuss when he would like your cat to be brought in to be neutered. You'll notice that I say "when," not "if," about this operation. It isn't an optional operation—next to providing the proper shots, food, water, and shelter, this is the single most important thing that you can do for a cat. There is not a single good argument against it, and many for: in addition to preventing further tragic feline overpopulation, the operation assures your cat, male or female, of a healthier, happier, stress-free life as a pet. From a selfish standpoint, if you need further convincing, only an altered male or spayed female cat can be a really pleasant and devoted pet—the single-minded behavior of a female in heat or a randy tomcat is not particularly pleasant to live with. Contrary to myth, neutering doesn't make a cat fat—overfeeding does.

Females are usually spayed before they come into their first heat, or estrus, although the operation can be successfully done at any age. The old theory that it was best to allow a female to have one litter before spaying simply isn't true—the ideal time is before sexual maturity makes the operation more complex. This is usually around five to six months of age. Some cats reach sexual maturity unusually early and come into

121

heat very young, however, and it's important that the operation not be performed during a heat period since it can be much more difficult then. If your doctor finds that your cat is in heat, unbeknown to you, he'll probably recommend waiting a week or so to do the operation. Don't worry that your pet will become a child-mother—if she should become pregnant accidentally, the spaying operation will take care of it. It's not unheard of, by the way, for a mistake to be made about a young kitten's sex, so be sure that you or the doctor double-check just to be sure. (This actually happened to a young tomcat belonging to a friend, and he underwent an unnecessary abdominal incision before the error was discovered, much to everyone's embarrassment!) In case you don't know: under the tail of a male are two dots like a colon, while a female has what looks like an upside-down exclamation point.

Since spaying is an abdominal operation, a general anesthetic must be used, and the doctor will usually tell you not to feed your pet for at least twelve hours before the procedure to avoid severe vomiting. Your cat's tummy will be shaved for the operation, and it will probably take at least a day (or overnight) for her to recover sufficiently to be allowed to go home. The size of the incision varies, but in young kittens it is very small (about a half inch) and will be stitched closed. It's a good idea to inspect the incision every day—if you see any redness, swelling, or discharge, call your doctor.

Altering a male cat, a much simpler procedure, is done by castration, or removal of the testes. As with females, male cats can be neutered at any age, but the operation is easier if it's performed at about six to eight months. Nowadays some veterinarians recommend waiting until a young male shows signs of maturity, to give the urethral passages time to reach their full size, and thereby hoping to prevent possible obstructions later in life. The proper age will vary with each individual, so be sure to consult with your doctor in advance. With older males veterinarians usually suggest operating during a period of no sexual activity, which generally occurs during the late fall and early winter. A general anesthetic is used for this operation,[1] so the same restrictions apply about eating beforehand. The operation is very short and uncomplicated, and the cat is almost always ready to return home the same day. The small incisions are not stitched but are left open; you should check them daily until they heal for any signs of infection. One good hint, given to me by my veterinarian the last time I had a cat neutered, is to use shredded newspaper instead of clay litter in your newly altered male's pan for a day or two, or until the wounds are closed, since small grains of litter can get into the openings and cause infection.

Both male and female cats will be a little dopey and wobbly when they come home from being neutered and should be given a quiet room in which to "sleep it off" undisturbed. If your postoperative cat will be sleeping on upholstered furniture or a bed, a rubber sheet or lots of thick toweling will protect against any bleeding or leakage of urine, which can occur while a cat is still partially anesthetized. A litter box, water, and a little favorite food should be nearby, and the patient should be left alone until he or she feels like company. Most young cats are completely recovered and back to their old selves a few days after the operation, but rough play should be avoided for several weeks. Follow your veterinarian's advice about when it's wise to let an outdoor cat have some freedom again.

Declawing

This is an operation that is entirely optional and extremely controversial. Unlike neutering, declawing is performed entirely for the benefit of the owner, not the pet. When you hear the arguments put forth by people who are strongly against it, you wonder why anyone even considers declawing. They state that declawing not only is physically very painful for a cat, but also results in permanent psychological damage. Most often, they say, the cat's personality changes completely after declawing: she becomes distrustful, nervous, and apt to bite.

On the other hand, some responses to a *Family Circle* column I wrote on declawing give a different picture: "We tried everything to train our cat not to scratch the furniture, and thought we'd have to get rid of her. In desperation, after researching it thoroughly, we declawed her. You can't imagine the difference in our relationship with our cat! In the past four years, we have had nothing to scold her for, and she's still the same affectionate, playful animal as before." "We declawed three years ago, and today Tai is even more affectionate than before. She has not become a biter. The only thing that's changed is that she no longer claws our furniture to shreds." "My cat has never shown any signs of being unhappy without front claws. He's able to jump and climb onto anything he wants, and gets down by himself."

Another reader pointed out that there are situations in which declawing is the only answer to cat ownership. She told of a paralyzed woman she knew whose cat had taken to climbing up her legs, inflicting serious scratches. Declawing solved her problem, as it has that of many ill or elderly people who couldn't keep a cat otherwise.

124

There's no doubt that the best solution to a scratching problem is training. But there are owners who are unable to train their cats, and there are also untrainable cats. (I know that some will say that this isn't true, but for practical purposes, it is.) Many owners have discovered that some very active breeds are likely to be particularly destructive with their claws, and very persistent in their refusal to be trained. When your furniture is rapidly disintegrating under Tabby's assaults, it's very difficult to care about her. If declawing is the only thing standing between your cat and the pound, it's one hundred to one the cat would opt for declawing if asked.

It's an operation that should never be done automatically. It's certainly not a pleasant experience for a cat to undergo, and is completely irreversible. Cats who are going to be allowed outdoors unsupervised shouldn't be declawed for safety reasons. Although declawed cats *can* climb using their hind claws, they're not as agile as their clawed siblings. In addition, while cats often fight with teeth and hind legs, they do use their front claws to fend off larger or fiercer animals, and a declawed cat will be at a great disadvantage in a real battle.

As with any operation, the younger the patient, the easier the procedure. But this is often not practical with declawing, since most owners aren't ready to resort to the operation until they've exhausted all other possibilities. If you know that you're going to declaw for some reason, though, the best time to do it is when you have your cat neutered.

Before you decided to declaw, read all that you can about it and discuss it with a veterinarian. Get several opinions if possible. It's very important that this operation be done by a doctor who's experienced in the procedure, because if it's not performed correctly there can be complications. If your regular doctor hasn't had a number of successful declawing operations, ask him to recommend a surgeon who has.

Ask yourself some serious questions: Am I sure that I'll be able always to keep my cat indoors, or under close supervision outside? Have I really tried to train my cat to use a proper scratching post? If I don't declaw, will I seriously have to consider getting rid of my cat? Am I prepared to be tolerant and understanding if the operation does result in some personality changes?

If you've researched declawing thoroughly, thought carefully about it, and can answer ''yes'' to all of these questions, then perhaps you and your cat would benefit from a declawing operation.

How to Tell If Your Cat Is Ill

> Poor Hodge, the cat, fell ailing, his appetite had gone.
> —SARAH WINGATE TAYLOR
> ''Hodge and Doctor Johnson''

As I said before, if you can recognize signs that your cat is not feeling well, you may be able to prevent a serious illness or emergency situation from developing. Sometimes this isn't easy; nonemergency cat illnesses can often go on for quite a long time before you notice them. Most cats aren't complainers, and their basic modesty about bodily functions may prevent you from knowing anything's wrong. Many symptoms of feline ill health are subtle and tend to develop so gradually that owners hardly pay any attention. So even the best-loved cat can be sick for some time before the signs are finally recognized. A regular weekly grooming-checkup can often help you to spot trouble.

GENERAL SIGNS OF ILL HEALTH

These general signs aren't illnesses in themselves, but can be indications of a number of different problems. Any that persist, or a combination of any of them, call for professional consultation.

A cat's *general appearance* is always a good indication of her health or lack of it. A dull, rough-looking coat; red, watery, sunken eyes; and skin that has lost its elasticity all signify that the cat is not well.

Often the first sign is a *change in temperament or habits*. If a formerly affectionate, sociable cat starts to be unresponsive or appears to lose interest in people and things that usually please her, she's probably either sick or getting sick. An energetic, lively animal who suddenly becomes listless isn't well, and a cat who suddenly refuses to allow you to touch or pet her is probably in pain. Many cats will also hide when they're not feeling well.

Another manifestation of illness is a *change in appetite*, no matter how gradual. If the environment and diet remain the same, adult cats' eating habits usually vary very little. A sudden increase in appetite may mean that your cat has intestinal parasites. On the other hand, a decrease in food intake or a lack of interest in eating at all may indicate a number of problems. If there are no other symptoms, you can safely wait several days with an adult cat, but if there are other signs of illness, appetite changes should be reported to your doctor right away. Kittens under a year old shouldn't be allowed to go without nourishment for more than twenty-four hours.

A *change in water drinking habits* can also signify

illness. Watch particularly for a situation where a cat sits looking at her water dish for a long time, but seems unable to drink. She may not be able to swallow for some reason, or may have a urinary stoppage. Immediate action is needed in order to prevent dehydration. Excessive water drinking can have many causes, but the most common are kidney or bladder ailments, or urinary stoppages. All these conditions require immediate treatment.

Occasional *vomiting or diarrhea* can be caused by stress, hair balls, or injudicious eating, but if either goes on for more than twenty-four hours, you should suspect illness. If the vomitus or stool is bloody, if the vomiting or diarrhea is particularly violent or painful, or if they occur at the same time, seek help right away. If your cat is troubled by hair balls despite frequent grooming, consult your veterinarian about giving her mineral oil, petroleum jelly, or a commercial hair ball-prevention preparation.

Shivering or trembling may be simply due to temporary chilling or excitement, but if it's accompanied by any other symptoms, or persists, it can be a sign of pain or fever.

If you think that your cat may have a *fever*, take her temperature (see p. 142). If you're at all nervous about doing this, or don't know how, it's best to take your pet to the doctor. A normal cat's temperature ranges between 101 and 102.5 degrees F. A *lowered temperature* (under 100 degrees) indicates severe illness.

Repeated *sneezing or coughing, or a watery discharge* from a cat's nose or eyes usually means that she has an upper respiratory infection. If your adult cat seems to be in good spirits otherwise and hasn't lost her appetite, you probably needn't worry, but if she seems at all "off," prompt treatment can prevent secondary infections, which may be dangerous. Kittens should have immediate attention for any respiratory problems.

Of course you'll call the doctor if you notice any *lumps*, *bumps*, or *swelling*. If your cat starts to *limp* or *walk stiffly* or *strangely*, it can be an indication of abdominal pain or swelling.

SOME COMMON CAT ILLNESSES

Briefly, here are some of the more common cat illnesses not covered in other sections, their symptoms, and treatment. I've already discussed external parasites, skin care, eye and ear problems in Chapter 2, "Grooming." Wounds, fractures, and poisoning are covered in the next chapter, "Indoors-Outdoors."

Internal Parasites

There are many kinds of internal parasites that cats can have, but the most commonly found are: protozoa (toxoplasmas, coccidia); roundworms (ascarids); hookworms; and tapeworms.

General indications that a cat is suffering from intestinal parasites are: listlessness; sharp change in appetite; loss of weight; bloating; rough, dry coat; vomiting or diarrhea. You may see some segments of worms in your cat's feces or vomitus, or clustered around her anus, but these aren't always present.

Symptoms of worms often don't appear until there's a severe infestation. Since these parasites sap your cat's health and energy by using up needed blood and nutrients, it's particularly important to have cats with any symptoms, and young kittens, tested for worms before they become weakened by them.

Kittens are often born with roundworms, or contract them soon after birth from their mother's milk. Other kinds of worms can be picked up by eating raw food or infested prey, from infected fleas and lice, or from the feces of infected animals.

Cleanliness, preventing your pet from eating raw food or prey, and regular fecal examinations by your doctor are the best protection against a severe worm infestation. If you suspect that your cat may be suffering from intestinal parasites, take a fresh fecal sample to your veterinarian; only by microscopic examination can he determine just which type of parasite your cat has and prescribe the proper treatment. With appropriate medication, worms can be completely eliminated. Don't ever automatically give commercial worm preparations, especially to a kitten: they can do severe harm, particularly if a cat is already weakened by worms.

Upper Respiratory Infections

Upper respiratory infections are quite common among cats, especially when they've been around other cats. The germs are airborne and therefore very difficult to control.

Most of the more serious respiratory illnesses can be prevented by immunization, but even a vaccinated cat can develop pneumonia. Signs that a cold is turning into something more severe are: fever; depression; loss of appetite; thick discharges from nose or eyes; coughing; difficult or labored breathing. If your cat displays any of these signs, she should be seen by a doctor. Most veterinarians feel that cats fare better at home when they have a respiratory infection; they need a lot of loving care. With proper care and medication, most cats recover from upper respiratory infections, but it can take as long as several weeks.

Urinary Problems

There are several kidney and bladder disorders cats can have, but the most common and potentially dangerous urinary tract disorder is feline cystitis, urolithiasis, or feline urologic syndrome (FUS).

Veterinarians agree that there are a number of different causes of this problem, but the results are the same: painful, frequent urination due to "sand" in the urinary tract. In males particularly, when this condition is left untreated it can lead to a urinary blockage—a very serious, possibly fatal condition.

Signs that a cat is suffering from some kind of urinary system problem are: drinking a great deal of water, or inability to drink water at all; frequent, painful urination, or inability to urinate at all, resulting in straining; urinating in strange places; blood in the urine; pain or swelling in the abdomen, which is often indicated by a strange gait. Straining and frequent trips to the litter tray or outdoors are often interpreted as signs of constipation by owners, but may indicate urinary problems. If your cat exhibits any of these symptoms, or a combination of them, have her checked right away.

If your pet does develop urinary trouble, the doctor will probably prescribe some antibiotics to clear up any infection, and advise you about any needed change in diet. It's especially important that a cat who has exhibited any urinary or bladder symptoms drinks plenty of water; ask your veterinarian how to encourage this if your cat is not much of a water drinker. Despite your best efforts, cats with a tendency toward this problem often have recurrent attacks, so watch your pet carefully, and alert anyone who may be going to take care of her to do so. Prompt action can usually prevent an emergency situation from developing—if it

131

should, however, waste no time in getting your pet to the doctor. (See p. 175 for emergency measures if there's a delay getting to a veterinarian.)

Blood Diseases

There are basically three types of *anemia* common to cats: anemia due to blood loss from an accident or a heavy infestation of external or internal parasites; anemia caused by a bodily malfunction; and infectious anemia, transmitted by other cats or infected external parasites (fleas, lice, ticks).

Anemia results when red blood cells are destroyed, and can be definitely diagnosed only by a blood count. Signs that a cat may be suffering from anemia are: pale gums, tongue, nose, and toe pads; listlessness and loss of appetite; loss of weight; dull coat; licking of odd things such as windowpanes, walls, or cement walks. In advanced stages, anemia sufferers may lose their appetites completely, have no energy at all, and lose control over bladder and bowel functions. If left untreated, anemia will eventually result in death. In severe cases, a blood transfusion is needed in order to save a cat.

To treat an anemic cat, the veterinarian will first have to determine what the cause is. He may have to perform a number of tests to do this. Once diagnosed, anemia is often treated with antibiotics, vitamin-mineral supplements, and a highly nutritious diet. Home care is usually best for a cat recovering from anemia.

One cause of feline anemia can be the *feline leukemia virus (FeLV)*, which can make a cat susceptible to a number of serious illnesses by reducing the natural body defenses. The most common of these illnesses is cancer.

132

FeLV is contagious between cats, primarily by prolonged, direct contact. The virus is shed in saliva, urine, feces, and milk. If one cat in a household tests positive for FeLV, all other cats should be tested for the disease. Signs of FeLV can include difficulty in breathing, diarrhea, and weight loss. FeLV is diagnosed by means of a specific blood test. There is now a vaccine to protect cats against this dread disease.

Recently, a virus that attacks a cat's immune system like FeLV has been identified. Named *feline T-lymphotripic lentivirus* (FTLV), it is thought to be transmitted mainly via saliva. The symptoms of FTLV are similar to those of FeLV. No preventive vaccine has yet been developed for FTLV, but early detection and care may extend an affected cat's life.

Feline infectious peritonitis (FIP) is another incurable ailment for which no preventive vaccine has yet been developed. Like FeLV and FTLV, it also depresses a cat's immune system and can affect all parts of the body. Anemia, fever, loss of appetite, weight loss, and depression, can all be signs of FIP. The prognosis for a cat with FIP is poor, and treatment consists mainly of supportive care.

There is no evidence that FeLV, FTLV, or FIP can be transmitted to humans.

Endocrine Diseases

Although endocrine diseases were rarely seen in cats in the past, they have been showing up with more frequency in recent years. Very little is known about the causes of these diseases in cats.

Diabetes mellitus is not common in cats, but it can occur in older animals. Typically, a diabetic cat will be excessively thirsty and will urinate frequently. Left untreated, diabetes can eventually cause coma and death. If your older cat exhibits the symptoms of diabetes, a diagnosis can be made through blood and urine analysis. An owner of a diabetic cat must be willing and able to give daily insulin injections and monitor her pet carefully.

Cases of *hyperthyroidism* in middle- to older-aged cats have increased dramatically in the past ten years. Sudden weight loss accompanied by increased appetite, hyperactivity, and a rapid heart rate are the primary symptoms of the disease, which can eventually lead to heart failure. Hyperthyroidism is diagnosed by a specialized blood test. Treatment varies, according to the age and general physical condition of the cat.

When to Seek Professional Advice

If your cat is ailing, you may feel that you should observe her for a while before calling your veterinarian. In general, however, if your doctor is available for telephone calls, it's far better to call right away than to worry and fret and end up calling anyway. In addition, if you talk to a veterinarian about whatever it is that's concerning you, he can probably help you to make better observations by telling you just what to look for.

Some conditions will turn into emergencies if you let them go too long. No doctor likes to treat emergencies, so don't feel that you're imposing or wasting his time if you call about something troublesome. Most doctors would much rather be "bothered" with a call that turns out to be about nothing much than to have a life-or-death situation on their hands.

In addition to real emergencies (listed on p. 171–2), you should consult your veterinarian if:

- Any unusual condition or behavior lasts for more than forty-eight hours, no matter how seemingly mild.
- You can't figure out what's wrong with your pet, but know that something's bothering her.
- Your cat has a fever.

Unless you've had a great deal of experience with cats, don't attempt to "doctor" your cat at home without a veterinarian's advice, and *never* give any medication or drugs not prescribed for that specific cat and specific illness.

CALLING THE VETERINARIAN

When you call your veterinarian about a health problem, there are several things you can do to make the call more productive. Before calling, make a list of all your pet's symptoms, how long you've noticed them, and any other related information such as appetite, bowel and bladder functions, and so forth. Very often the doctor can't speak with you the minute you call and will have to return your call. If the situation isn't an emergency, several hours may sometimes go by before he can get back to you. Without a list near the phone, you may very well forget something important.

The same procedure is a great help when you take your cat to the doctor's office. Nine times out of ten, a cat won't act, or react, normally in a veterinarian's office, so it's important for you to be able to relate specific details of your pet's behavior and symptoms to the doctor. Observing your cat carefully and making notes before visiting or talking to the doctor will help him to make a much speedier and more accurate diagnosis then one based solely on seeing a frightened, ailing cat.

As soon as you reach the doctor on the phone, remind him briefly just what cat you're speaking of. You may have only one cat, but the veterinarian may have hundreds of feline patients. He can't be expected to remember "Susie" by name. Give him a brief description of your cat and remind him of any illnesses, medications, or treatments she's had. This will enable him to remember your cat more clearly than his charts and records will allow him to. Unless you know for sure from previous experience, don't attempt to diagnose your cat's trouble, but just give a rundown of her symptoms.

After talking to you and asking some questions, your doctor will do one of several things: he may think that it's advisable for you to bring your pet in for an examination; he may tell you to observe her closely for a day and call back; he may prescribe some simple steps for you to take at home, reporting the results; or he may tell you that whatever is troubling your cat is normal and will probably run its course and go away by itself. Don't expect a veterinarian to be able to diagnose a serious or complex illness over the phone, or to prescribe any drugs without seeing your cat.

Whatever the doctor tells you to do, be sure that you understand his instructions. Write them down if they're at all complicated. It's much easier for both of you to make sure that you clearly understand what you're to do the first time than to have to call back.

Caring for a Sick Cat at Home

Most veterinary hospitals have kind, animal-loving staffs who give the animals in their care as much attention and gentle treatment as they can. There are obvious situations when a cat must remain in the hospital: when she needs intravenous feeding or medication, transfusions, frequent surgical procedures, or many other specific kinds of care and treatment that only a veterinarian can perform. In some cases, however, your sick cat will fare much better at home than in the hospital.

Recently I left Wilbur overnight in the hospital for treatment of an abscess. He was there less than twenty-four hours, and it took him two weeks to recover—not from the abscess, which healed quickly, but from the overnight stay. He was scared and jumpy, and lost his appetite. His reaction was extreme, but if he ever has to have a minor operation again, I'll make a point of bringing him home as soon as possible and let the anesthetic wear off in familiar surroundings, with encouraging words from his human family.

Cats especially dislike strange places, distrust strangers, and hate being locked up in a cage. They can also become very depressed when they don't feel well, and often will simply give up without a great deal of tender loving care. Veterinarians know this and will often recommend home care if possible for certain kinds of illness.

They are less likely to favor home care for a postoperative cat or one who is wounded or hurt. Many owners aren't able to medicate, wash wounds, replace drains, or do other distasteful and messy jobs for their pets. In cases like this it's much better to keep a cat in the hospital until the worst part of the treatment is over. You shouldn't feel guilty about this. If you're nervous or apprehensive about treating your cat at home, you'll be a poor nurse anyway. As I've said many times, cats can sense immediately if you're nervous or unsure, and the combination of a tentative owner trying to treat an uncooperative cat will result in chaos, and possibly in a much sicker cat. For instance, a friend whose cat was recently badly injured by a car couldn't bear to look at him until his stitches had all been removed and his wounds partially healed. Her veterinarian knew her well enough to keep her cat in the hospital until he was presentable. She could never have dressed his wounds.

If you think that you do want to treat an ailing cat at home, you'll have to consider several things. In addition to being willing and able to medicate or dress wounds, you should have some time to spend with your pet. If you're going to put your sick cat alone in a closed room and visit her twice a day, she'd probably be better off with hospital care. A sick or hurt cat needs a lot of attention in order to get well.

Other important considerations in home care are your relationship with your cat and your pet's particular temperament. Home care probably won't work for a very nervous, bad-tempered, or extremely hand-shy cat. If you have difficulty handling your cat even when she's well, and have to fight with her in order to do routine grooming chores, then you shouldn't attempt to care for her when she's not feeling well. A testy cat will become even testier when she's ailing, and it may take more than one expert pair of hands to deal with her. If you're at all frightened of your cat and don't trust her not to bite or scratch, don't try home care. She's better off with the calm, competent handling of professionals. You and your cat must trust each other absolutely for home care to work well.

Even gentle, loving, trusting cats can be difficult when they're ill. Cats generally are not good or cooperative patients. They resent not feeling well, and owners often get the feeling that their cat blames them for their discomfort. Ailing cats will often make absolutely no effort to help themselves, but seem to become dispirited and give up completely. They have to be coaxed to eat and drink, to use a litter tray, and even to keep themselves clean. It's well to remember, too, that pain and discomfort can cause your pet's personality to change temporarily. Your formerly loving, trusting cat may become suspicious, wary, and cantankerous. You'll have to try not to take it personally and lose patience with your pet. Even a cat who's not seriously ill may require a great deal of loving, patient care to get better.

You may also have to prove to your doctor that you can care for your pet properly at home. After demonstrating any procedures that it will be necessary to do, he may want to see you do them yourself. Don't be upset by this precaution—many people find that once they get home, they either can't remember how to proceed, or are afraid to do certain things. Something that looks very easy when an expert does it can prove to be very difficult when you're new at it.

THE SICKROOM

Once you and your veterinarian have decided that your cat can be well cared for at home, you'll need to prepare a sickroom. It's best to keep an ailing cat confined when you're not prepared to supervise her, but if she's not very ill you may want to give her the run of the house when you're around. Sick cats tend to want to hide and will often squeeze themselves into tiny, hard-to-get-at places, under floorboards, or up on high shelves. I once heard a terrible story about a badly wounded cat whose owners thought she'd run away because they couldn't find her. Months later, they found her body wedged under a very low, heavy dresser in the attic. If your pet must be kept very quiet, you can line a carton or box with toweling and place a window screen on top to keep her from trying to move around. Needless to say, a sick cat shouldn't be allowed outdoors alone.

The sickroom should be quiet and warm. If there are drafts, you can rig up a temporary screen around your pet by draping blankets or towels over chairs or cartons. If you use a portable heater in the room, be sure that it's placed high up, well out of a cat's reach—a feverish cat may try to lie too close to it and get burned. It's important for a sick cat to know that the people she knows and loves are around, but don't let small children and other pets bother her. Just as you would for a sick human, confine visits to short, quiet stays.

Leaving the door of the room ajar when you're at home will allow your cat to hear familiar household noises and, when she's feeling better, to venture out on her own. As soon as your pet is starting to recover, she'll probably have the normal cat reaction to being closed in—irritation or even panic.

She should have a warm, soft place off the floor to sleep. If she'll be resting on upholstered furniture or a bed, a rubber sheet or several layers of towels will protect the surface against accidents.

A litter tray should be near your cat's sleeping place. A very sick cat may not be able to get to the litter tray by herself, so you many have to lift her into it at regular intervals. If she should make a mistake, don't make a big deal out of it, she'll be upset enough. Be sure to clean the tray more frequently than usual because illness can make cats very fussy and sensitive. Baking soda mixed with the litter can help absorb bad odors.

Your sick cat may not be strong enough to even keep herself clean. You can help remove loose fur by soft brushing if she's well enough, or by wiping your cat gently with a washcloth dampened with warm water.

She may need to have her faced washed, and matter removed from her eyes and nose with a cloth or moistened cotton swab. If she has diarrhea or has temporarily lost control of her bladder or bowels, clean that area several times a day with warm water and mild soap, if needed. A little mineral oil or Vaseline will help to soothe irritated skin. Some baking soda rubbed into her fur will help her smell fresh. A really sick cat who can't move should be turned over several times a day to prevent bed sores. If your cat develops sores or lesions anywhere, check with your doctor about what to use to soothe and heal them.

Nourishment

Clean, fresh water should be nearby, and small amounts of food if your cat is able to eat by herself. It's extremely important for a sick cat to drink plenty of water and eat, so that she won't become dehydrated and weak. Sick cats often lose all interest in eating and drinking, so you may have to coax, or even force, your pet to take liquid and nourishment. Start by offering a favorite food in your hand. If your cat eats, feed only a small amount at a time so that she doesn't get sick, and repeat at frequent intervals.

If she can't take solid food, try offering some broth or strained foods, such as baby foods. You can force-feed small amounts of soft food or liquids, such as egg yolk or milk if your cat can tolerate it, with a spoon, by placing the spoon against the side of your pet's mouth behind her large teeth, and pouring in a little at a time. Don't ever try to force food or liquid down a cat's throat or you may choke her! Start with very little, and if your cat vomits, stop immediately, and try again later. A large medicine dropper or syringe, placed in the same spot at the side of the mouth,

141

can be used to give liquid nourishment and water when a cat is too sick to eat and drink. Follow your veterinarian's advice about how much to give, and when it's safe to try to graduate to solid foods.

The doctor may want you to keep an accurate record of your pet's daily food and water intake. It's a good idea to keep a pad and pencil handy, anyway, to record other data such as temperature, and so forth.

Taking a Cat's Temperature

Your doctor will probably want a daily report on your cat's temperature. Whether she has a fever is often a sign of how her illness or infection is progressing.

Taking a cat's temperature isn't difficult, but it does require calmness and determination on your part. You should use a large-bulbed rectal thermometer rather than the thinner, more fragile kind. Before starting, lubricate the tip with some Vaseline or vegetable oil, and shake the thermometer down below 100 degrees. With your cat standing on a hard surface, put your arm around her body, holding her against you, and lift up her tail. If your cat's very ill, she can be lying on her side, but it's easier if she's standing. Push the thermometer into her rectum firmly, twisting it a little if necessary. Cats have very strong sphincters, and you may feel quite a bit of resistance. Continue to push, gently but firmly, until the thermometer is inserted about one to two inches. Your cat may protest loudly, but don't worry—it really doesn't hurt. Leave the thermometer in for two minutes, while you continue to hold your cat so that she can't sit down or run away. The first few times you take your cat's temperature, you may want to restrain her with a towel wrapping, or have someone help you keep her still.

Medicating

Pills, capsules, and liquid medicines should go directly into the cat, not into food or water unless they're specifically designed to do so. If your cat's off her feed, you can't be sure that the entire dose will be taken in food. Also, many medicines are designed to dissolve and go to work in the stomach or intestinal tract, and won't be as effective when mixed with food or water.

Liquid medicines are easy to give by dropper or syringe directly into your cat's mouth. As with forced feeding, don't pour liquids down a cat's throat, but squirt them into her mouth from the side, behind her long teeth.

Have your doctor show you how to give your cat a pill or capsule. No written instructions can take the place of a demonstration, which I just discovered after many years of trying to follow them. However, here goes. With your cat on a hard surface, put one hand over the top of her head, covering her ears, with finger and thumb resting on either side of her head. Holding the pill in your other hand, tilt her head back, and pry her front teeth apart with the tip of your finger. Place the pill on the back of the cat's tongue in the valley, or dent, that you see there, and give it a little shove down her open throat with your finger. Some books advocate using a pencil eraser for this final shove, but I can't figure out how you can hold a pencil in the hand that must pry open the cat's mouth and hold the pill, too—unless you have a helper. You can lubricate a large pill or capsule with vegetable oil, if you wish.

The secret, which I just found out, is to tilt the cat's head way back, creating a clear, straight passage in her throat for the pill to go down. The other secret is to act very quickly and surely before she can realize what's going on and struggle. If you don't do the whole thing very fast, even a good-natured cat will have time to fight back. Don't allow yourself to be put off by your cat's moans or groans of protest. Grit your teeth and proceed with dispatch. As it was explained to me, the element of surprise combined with the well-tilted head means you can't miss—well, hardly ever. If you do miss, your cat will now be alerted, and you may have to wait awhile before there's another opportune moment to catch her by surprise.

If the pill doesn't go all the way down, your cat will probably spit it right out, and you'll have to try again later. I've never been able to figure out why they can't make pills for animals that don't taste awful, but they can't seem to. That's another good reason, by the way, for not giving a pill mixed in food; the bad taste and smell will warn your cat off.

When you've had success giving your cat one pill, you'll find out that it's not really as hard as it sounds.

Restraints

If you're not quick enough, or your cat's really suspicious, she may try to fend you off with her front paws when you try to medicate her. Painful or unpleasant treatment of wounds, especially in the head area, may meet with the paw defense, too. If your cat really fights with her claws, you may have to restrain her in order to medicate her, otherwise you'll turn the whole thing into a messy, ineffective battle.

There are a couple of ways to restrain a cat, both of which rely on surprise for real success. Approaching your cat from the rear, quickly wrap her, legs and all, in a bath towel or sweater, or pop a sleeveless armhole over her head, winding the cat securely in the garment. The trick is to be sure that all her legs are wrapped tightly. If her strong back legs are left free, your cat is likely to use them to kick and struggle free, and may scratch you badly. Unless you have an assistant to hold the wrapping tightly, you'll then have to hold your cat against you in your lap, or on a table or counter with your arm tightly around her. If you have to medicate other parts of a cat's body, you may find that you have to bind her legs loosely if you're working alone.

It's really difficult to muzzle a cat, but you may want to try if you have a biting animal to work on. Taking a strip of soft cloth or rope, wind it firmly around the cat's jaw and nose from top to bottom, then bring the ends around the back of her neck behind the ears, cross them, wind them around her body, and tie them under her chest behind her front legs. This is really hard to do, and the muzzle shouldn't be left on for more than a few minutes, always under close supervision, so that the cat doesn't choke herself trying to get loose. It should only be used in extreme situations—it's really much better to simply have someone hold the cat's jaw closed. Another defense against a biting cat is to have a helper hold her tightly by the loose skin at the top of her neck so that she can't turn around and bite. Shaking a cat's head while holding on to the nape of her neck can help to distract her.

If you want to prevent your cat from biting or licking part of her body, or from being able to scratch her head, you can put an "Elizabethan collar" on her. She'll hate it, but it will keep her from getting her mouth close enough to pull out stitches or continually lick an area. It will also keep her hind legs away from her head. Take a large piece of stiff paper or cardboard and cut a circle in it just large enough for your cat's neck. Then cut a straight line from the outside edge to the neck hole, place it around your cat's neck just

145

behind the ears, and Scotch-tape the straight cut. Your pet will have trouble sleeping in this arrangement, so don't leave it on any longer than necessary.

Convalescence

If your cat has had a hospital stay, don't expect her to be able to plunge right back into normal household activities when she gets home. She'll probably be very tired and somewhat confused. It's a good idea to prepare a quiet place for her to rest in for a while until she's ready for company. Other pets may be aggressive or standoffish with a returnee at first because of her hospital smell. Let them sniff the carrier, which will probably have mixed hospital-home odors, to help reassure them that this is really their old friend.

Whether she's been cared for in the hospital or at home, as your cat becomes stronger, or better, she may want more freedom. Some illnesses take a long time to be completely cured, so don't let a false sense of well-being persuade you to let your cat resume her normal life-style too quickly. In some instances, the doctor may want to see your pet again before pronouncing her entirely fit. In others he may rely on your good judgment.

As with all convalescents, a serious illness or infection can make a cat much more susceptible to secondary infection, so you should take care that your recovering pet doesn't become overtired or isn't put into stressful situations for a while. Small children and other animals should be restrained from rough play, and your recuperating cat should continue to have a quiet place to retreat to when she needs it.

Sometimes cats who have been extremely ill need coaxing to start leading a normal, unprotected life again. They have been so traumatized by their illness

146

that they need to be reintroduced to the world around them very gently and slowly. If your pet shows signs of extreme nervousness or reluctance to leave the sickroom after she's on her way to recovery, you'll have to be very patient and understanding and allow her to become reacquainted with the outside world gradually.

Notes—Chapter 5

1. Formerly required only for cats over six months, a general anesthetic is now legally mandated at any age, no matter how young. See Joan O. Joshua, F.R.C.V.S., *Cat Owner's Encyclopedia of Veterinary Medicine*, T.F.H. Publications, Neptune, N.J., 1977.

6

Indoors-Outdoors

Curiosity may have killed the cat; more
likely the cat was just unlucky.
            —ALISTAIR REID, "Curiosity"

Cats are probably the most adaptable of all the domestic animals that people keep as pets. As long as
they're with humans they care for, most cats are able
to live contentedly in almost any setting.

One of the things that often recommends cats to
people as desirable pets is their ability to spend their
entire lives indoors perfectly happily. Cats' space requirements are small; they don't need a great deal of
exercise and can usually manage to get what they do
crave even in a relatively small apartment. They sleep
a lot, and are able to amuse themselves perfectly well
indoors with some help. They're gentle and quiet—
except for some of the more vocal breeds, cats won't
disturb even the closest neighbors (although we once
had a Siamese living in a next-door apartment whose
cries of protest every time she was left alone could
have been heard around the block!). In addition, cats
are tidy and clean; they even can come to you already
litter-box trained. In short, cats are the ideal city or
apartment-dweller's pet.

Cats are also good suburban and country pets. When they're allowed outdoors, neutered cats will seldom roam very far, but prefer to stay within sight, or perhaps scent, of home territory. They readily adapt themselves to regular routines, appearing on the doorstep promptly at suppertime and bedtime, for instance.

From Inside to Out and Vice Versa

Some cats are even able to go with their owners on visits, switching from one life-style to another with equanimity—spending winters indoors in a city apartment, for instance, and summering with freedom outdoors in the country or suburbs. Others find it harder to accommodate. When we were first married, my husband and I lived in a city apartment. We had a big gray cat named Jeffrey. On summer weekends we often went to the country to visit my parents, taking Jeffrey with us. Once there, he loved to go outdoors, climbing trees and chasing things. Somehow he always sensed when we were getting ready to go back to the city. He'd go down to the cellar and get as far back as he could into a narrow crawl space under the porch. He couldn't ever be coaxed out, and my husband would end up having to "belly" into the crawl space to drag Jeffrey out. Once in his carrier, he seemed resigned to the trip home, and resumed his seemingly contented life back in the apartment until the next time he went to the country and to a life-style he obviously preferred.

When it's necessary, cats can change life-styles completely, but it may take them some time to adjust. A young, active cat who's spent most of her waking hours racing around outdoors may have some difficulty adapting to life in a small apartment, but she can do it with your help. She'll need lots of toys for climbing and exercise, regular rough-and-tumble play with you, and possibly a companion to run around with. You'll have to take care to see that she doesn't get into trouble poking into things, and be especially watchful about open windows and doors she might escape through at first. As your active cat gets older, she'll gradually calm down and soon will be perfectly content in her new indoor home.

Taking a cat who has lived her entire life in the confines of four walls and suddenly giving her outdoor freedom is another matter. Unless your pet's very young, or originally came from the country, she may surprise you by being very wary when faced with an open door. Unlike Jeffrey, whose weekend visits to the country had given him a taste of freedom that he enjoyed, many cats who have spent their lives in an apartment seem to prefer the safety of the indoors to the lure of grass and trees. You can help your pet adjust by continuing to provide her with a litter box in the house, so that she doesn't have to go out if she doesn't want to, and by accompanying her outdoors the first few times to "protect" her. She may never venture any farther away than the doorstep if she's an older cat, and there's no reason why you should ever force her to go out if she really doesn't want to. Most cats will learn to enjoy the outdoors once they've overcome their initial fear of freedom, however.

The Indoor Cat

He prowls the tropic warmth from door to
door and stares through his transparent
walls of glass. . . .
—ULRICH TROUBETZKOY,
"Indoor Jungle Blues"

Caring for Your Cat's Physique

Most people agree that it's really not at all unkind always to keep a cat indoors. In fact, a great many cat lovers feel strongly that every cat should be kept safely inside all of the time, no matter where one lives. Their view is that it's cat owners' responsibility to keep their pets safe from cars, parasites, strange animals, and all the other dangers a cat could meet up with abroad. Since cats can adapt perfectly happily to life inside, they ask, why take the risk of ever allowing them outdoors?

If you live in an apartment or a city, there's little question that your cat will probably stay inside for her entire life. Even in some suburban or country settings, proximity to roads and other dangers may make it obvious that you shouldn't let your cat go out. And, if you own a valuable pedigreed animal, you probably won't want to take a chance on her being lost or stolen. From a practical standpoint, it can be less costly in the long run to have a completely indoor cat—if your pet's not exposed to certain diseases she'll need fewer shots.

Just keeping your cat inside the house won't prevent her from getting into any trouble, however. Some young cats seem to have a penchant for getting into everything. Their exploits are often attributed to curiosity, but boredom and restlessness are actually the main reasons why cats get themselves into scrapes indoors. It's especially important for young indoor cats to have plenty of acceptable things to do to keep them out of trouble. While it's true that cats do sleep a great deal, youngsters are usually raring to go the minute they wake up. You should provide your indoor cat with a number of things to entertain herself with when you're not around to play with her. Climbing toys are excellent outlets for excess energy, for instance (see Chapter 3).

151

A very active daily play session with you can also help use up some of your young cat's pep; she can practice her pouncing and stalking techniques on you instead of the furniture. If your cat is alone a lot, she'll soon learn to anticipate a regular playtime with you.

Another pet to play with can be very good for a cat who's often left alone indoors, but remember that two young cats can get into twice as much mischief as one. It's best to wait until your kitten grows up a bit before getting another kitten for her to play with (see "New Pets" in Chapter 9).

GETTING INTO TROUBLE INDOORS

Just as you'd child-proof a house if needed, you should kitten-proof the rooms your indoor pet will have free access to. I've already talked about the dangers of electric-cord chewing (p. 32), and should add that kittens seem to have an uncanny ability to find small things even when you can't. Watch out for needles, pins, thumbtacks, coins, rubber bands, and tiny toys. Older cats seem to know enough to leave these things alone, but kittens will often swallow them and either choke or stop up their insides.

Poisoning Indoors

In addition to swallowing objects that can stick inside them, cats and kittens can accidentally swallow poison. Adult cats aren't very likely to eat or drink anything that is obviously poisonous because of their highly developed sense of smell and taste. But they do become accidentally poisoned in three primary ways: licking a poisonous substance off their fur or feet (paint, turpentine, garden chemicals); eating or drinking something poisonous that smells or tastes good (antifreeze, poisoned prey, some furniture polishes); and nipping or biting something poisonous that has no particularly strong smell or taste (for instance, plant parts).

Kittens are often less fastidious than older cats, and their discriminatory sense isn't as highly developed. Kittens will chew on cigarette butts, and will often stick their noses into household cleaners or insecticides. Usually they won't ingest enough of any of these things to make them seriously ill, but they can irritate or burn their mouths, noses, and throats before you can stop them.

A great deal has been written about houseplants that can be poisonous for cats to chew on or eat. The list of poisonous plants is very long, and I won't rerun it here—the safest rule is not to let your cat chew on any plants. The ingesting of small parts of most household plants is rarely fatal and usually results in only minor discomfort such as a rash or mouth irritation, but some plants, such as dieffenbachia (or dumb cane), can cause temporary paralysis of the throat and vocal cords; others, like Jerusalem cherry, can bring on severe stomach pain, diarrhea, and dizziness. Chewing on the leaves or stems of philodendron plants can make a cat's throat and tongue swell enough to cause asphyxiation. What may not occur to you is that even if a plant is out of reach, the leaves and berries do drop off and can land where a cat can get at them. The plump red fruit of the Jerusalem cherry, for instance, can be an intriguing plaything; I recently caught Wilbur, who's trained not to go near plants, batting around a big red Jerusalem cherry. So shake your plants gently from time to time so that you can collect loose berries and leaves and throw them away before your cat finds them.

Bored cats or kittens sometimes lick things, such as

153

furniture or bric-a-brac, getting a small amount of polish or glue into their systems. It's also possible for a cat to eat little bits of houseplants or other things undetected, over a period of time. If you notice that your pet seems listless, drools a lot, trembles involuntarily, or has chronic diarrhea or vomiting, she could be poisoning herself gradually. If you suspect that your cat may have been poisoned, waste no time in getting her to the doctor (see emergency treatment for poisoning, p. 176).

Getting Closed In

Cats will often slip unseen into closets, cupboards, or closed rooms or attics, where they may not be discovered for hours or even days. No matter where they are in the house, our two cats seem to always know when someone's going up into the attic, which they love for some reason. No one ever sees them go through the door, but invariably when one is missing at suppertime or bedtime, somebody will remember having gone up to the attic for a minute. Sure enough, when the door's opened, there's Wilbur or Francis, waiting to be let out again.

Not long ago we were waiting at a boarding gate in a New York airport. All of a sudden, a woman nearby jumped up and went hurriedly to the nearest telephone. Returning, she laughingly explained to us that she'd been calling her cat-sitter in Connecticut—she'd just realized that one of her cats, who'd been missing that morning, was probably closed in a kitchen cupboard. She had a vague recollection of seeing the cat go into the cupboard the night before, and had just thought of it. She was afraid that if she didn't call the sitter, the poor cat might not be found for days. (Some cats will call to be let out of places, but many have such soft voices that, unless you're listening for it, you may not hear them.)

Small kittens are especially likely to get into things unnoticed. I'll never forget when two of Grace's kittens narrowly escaped suffocation. I was in the kitchen getting dinner ready the day after Thanksgiving, and the two very small, barely weaned kittens were hanging around, intrigued by the smell of turkey. We sat down to eat, and soon one of the children got up to get himself more milk. He opened the refrigerator and there, sitting on the bottom shelf next to the turkey, were the two little kittens! They were pretty chilly, but otherwise no worse for wear. Obviously they'd slipped into the refrigerator just as the door was closing, and no one had seen them. They were very lucky to be discovered quickly. A less lucky kitten belonging to a friend was accidentally "dried" to death with some clothes; he'd apparently gotten into the machine and fallen asleep when she wasn't looking.

If you're aware of this penchant for getting into things, you'll remember to keep your eyes open for a flash of tail as you close a door, and you'll know where to check if your pet turns up missing. Be sure that you *see* your cat before you go out for any length of time.

Too Much Heat

Some cats love warmth almost as much as they do getting into things unnoticed. They often seem to be oblivious to overheating and even to singed fur. Many cats regularly sleep on or under radiators, or over the pilot light on the top of a gas stove. For some reason, most seem to be able to avoid getting burned. Randolph and Patrick, two Rex cats belonging to a friend, sit on top of her gas stove all of the time. (Rex cats in particular crave warmth because of their thin coats.) Their owner finally had to put a thick, heavy wooden cutting board over the stove top when she wasn't around, to be sure that the cats didn't burn themselves. In *The Cat*, Muriel Beadle tells of one woman who poured thick syrup all over the top of her stove to discourage her cats from "stove-top lounging." The author concludes that in this case the cure seems worse to her than the bad habit it's meant to stop.

Fires in fireplaces can be fascinating for kittens, and they sometimes seem to be unaware of any danger. I've seen kittens who acted as if they were going to walk right into the edge of a roaring fire until they were grabbed. If you're going to leave a kitten alone in the room with a fire going, be absolutely sure there's a sturdy screen in front of it. It's often very hard to tell if a cat's burn is serious or not—blisters sometimes don't form because of the fur. If your cat has been burned, it's a good idea to consult a veterinarian even though the burn doesn't look bad to you.

The habit of sleeping in excessively warm places can be bad for a cat's general health, too. Pong used to like to sleep in the uninsulated attic of our summer house on very hot days, until the veterinarian told us not to allow him to do it anymore. It seems that too much heat can dehydrate a cat's skin and mucous membranes. So, although it's not really dangerous to allow your cat to sleep on radiators and other very hot places (it's hard to prevent it altogether), try to discourage her from excessive self-roasting.

Falls from Windows

All cats, even those who go outdoors, love to look out of windows, and will often spend hours sitting on a sill peering out. If the window's open and a bird or butterfly goes past, a cat may forget that she's ten stories up. Apparently cats also lack depth perception and have no way of judging long distances. Unfortunately, it simply isn't true that cats are so sure-footed that they never fall. Falls by cats from open apartment windows are so common that city veterinarians call it the "high-rise syndrome." And, although there have been cases of cats who survived twenty-story falls, contrary to myth cats don't always land on their feet unharmed when they fall long distances.

Don't assume that your cat knows enough not to step out an open window. Unless you live on the ground floor, be sure that any window you're going to open is securely screened, or open all your windows from the top.

The Indoor-Outdoor Cat

> When you let him in, then he wants to be
> out;
> He's always on the wrong side of every
> door.
> —T. S. ELIOT, "The Rum Tum Tugger"

Except for Jeffrey, who later became one, we've always had indoor-outdoor cats. They go in and out all day long when anyone's at home to be a doorman, and are always waiting on one side of some door or another to be let through the minute anyone comes home. Sometimes Wilbur is in and wants to go out, while at the same time Francis is on the other side of the same

157

door wanting in. I used to leave the back door ajar in nice weather so that they could come and go at will. I stopped doing that when Francis brought a live bird into the house one spring day.

I doubt that there are many people living in the city now who let their cats outdoors, but years ago, when I lived in a city house with a back yard, our family cats used to go out. Long before anyone else had one, we had a pet trapdoor installed in our basement door. Pong soon learned how to use the trapdoor by pushing it to go out, and lifting it with a paw or his nose to let himself in. One night, however, we came home to be confronted by two huge, mangy tomcats sitting in the living room while Pong crouched on a chair back looking nervous. We finally got our visitors to leave, and from then on kept the door hooked when we were going to be out so that Pong's "friends" couldn't come in.

So much for making life easier for yourself with a self-serve door for your indoor-outdoor cat—you take the risk of finding various kinds of unwelcome visitors in your house. It's usually best to resign yourself to being a doorman for your pet.

Why bother letting your cat out at all? Well, in addition to eliminating the fuss of litter pans, there are several reasons. Our family spends a great deal of time outdoors, and we've always enjoyed having our pets with us when they wanted to be. What's more, our cats thoroughly enjoy being outside: they sit in the sun, run in the grass, climb trees, and chase things. They rarely get into any serious difficulty because they don't wander far from home.

We've never seen Wilbur or Francis go any farther away than the next house. The only time that either of them ventures down the road is to take a stroll with the dogs and us. Wilbur started this routine, and now

Francis sometimes joins him. It's really a very funny sight: as soon as someone starts out the door with a dog on a leash, Wilbur appears from somewhere around the house and walks right along with us, pausing to investigate under bushes and behind trees, and then trotting to catch up. As soon as we turn around to go home, he follows and comes right back with us.

Like most indoors-outdoor cats, Wilbur and Francis always show up without fail for supper and for a bedtime snack. We've always preferred to keep our cats indoors at night, but Francis hates to stay in except in very bad weather. He usually makes our lives so miserable, pacing and meowing, that we give in and let him out most nights. In the morning, he's always sitting on the doorstep waiting for breakfast.

> My cat jumps to the windowsill and sits
> there still as a jug.
> —MAY SWENSON, "Waiting for *It*"

Wilbur has another habit I used to think was unique. When he's outdoors and wants to be let in, he somehow knows just which room of the house to come to. If I'm in an upstairs bedroom, he suddenly appears on the windowsill, fifteen feet off the ground. If someone's in the kitchen, it's that sill he jumps to; and if I'm in my little office on the ground floor, all of a sudden I see his face peering in at me through that window. He's even taught Francis this trick, and sometimes there they both are, looking in the window and meowing to be let in!

As I say, I thought that this was unique until a friend who has three cats told me that Helen, Eustace, and Schuyler not only know what window to come to to be let in, but also scratch for attention. She says that her cats' window scratchings are each somewhat different so that she can always tell which one's outside without even looking.

Even though I now know that this trick isn't Wilbur's invention, I'm still amazed by it. I wonder how these cats know what room to go to? Do they wander from sill to sill, starting with the easiest one, or do they simply take a chance? I've never seen them do the rounds of windowsills, so I can only assume that they can either hear, or smell, well enough to know what room someone's in. Our cats never go to any of the windows in rooms that are used rarely, but they do seem to know as soon as one of our sons comes home, and his windowsill then becomes a "let-me-in" perch, too. However they do it, and no matter how busy anyone is, we stop and let the cat in right away. After all, if he's gone to all that trouble to find us, he deserves prompt service.

GETTING INTO TROUBLE OUTDOORS

Because our cats don't go very far afield, they rarely get into much trouble outdoors. There used to be some dogs in our neighborhood who chased cats, but now that the leash law is more strictly enforced, we've had no trouble with cat-hating dogs in many years. Once in a while a new cat or a stray will come along, and there'll be some territorial fighting for a few days, but it usually seems to resolve itself quite fast. Outdoor cats *can get* themselves into difficulty, however.

Hunting

> They call me cruel. Do I know if a mouse
> or songbird feels?
> —C. S. CALVERLY, "The Cat"

One possible problem of the outdoor cat isn't easy to resolve. Even if your cat roams no farther than your

160

neighbor's yard, if she's a bird-hunter she may not be a welcome visitor. While mouse- and rat-hunting are applauded by almost everyone, bird-hunting is considered variously as a nuisance or a crime.

Some cats never actually hunt birds. They'll sit inside a window staring out at them, like Wilbur, with tail twitching furiously, but outdoors their interest in birds seems to be confined just to watching. The predatory instinct in cats varies considerably, and there's no real way to know ahead of time whether your cat will grow up to be a hunter. However, kittens are taught to hunt by their mothers, so it's pretty safe to assume that if a mother cat is a real hunter, her kittens will be hunters, too.

Realists point out that even the most determined bird-hunting cat is able to catch very few birds. They say that a cat is generally no match for a healthy bird and that usually the only birds that can be caught are sick, old, or unfit; therefore, they reason that cats actually do an invaluable service by cutting down on bird overpopulation. This may be true in the wild, but if there's a bird feeder around with ground-feeding birds visiting it, a cunning cat is provided with pretty easy targets. It may not be easy to convince your bird-loving neighbor that your cat is doing the bird population a favor when she's just carried off the fifth bird in a week from underneath his feeder.

Even if you think that your cat is not being "bad" when she hunts birds, but is engaging in a perfectly natural activity, you may want to try to discourage her from bird-hunting to keep peace in your neighborhood. In the first place, tell your neighbor that you're trying to deal with the problem and invite him to help you. Suggest that he shoo the cat away every time he sees her nearby, instead of waiting for her to pounce on a bird. You could even arm him with a water pistol for this purpose. Belling your cat may make you both feel better, but in my experience birds don't seem to be frightened by bells, and the ringing may drive both you and your pet wild.

Most cats bring their catch to their humans for approval and praise. If your cat does this, it can be a big help in discouraging her from catching birds. When a cat brings prey home, she'll usually announce her arrival with loud calls, summoning her owners to come and see the wonderful thing she's done. As soon as you hear this recognizable calling, go out and immediately take the bird away from your cat at the same time telling her that she's a "bad girl." Since your cat is certainly not catching birds because she's hungry, by regularly taking all the "fun" out of bird-hunting you may be able to break her of the habit.

The most common prey for domestic cats is small rodents: mice, moles, and even rats make up the usual cat victim list. Owners are generally pleased when a cat brings home a rodent to show them and praise the cat for her skill. One thing that many people find offensive and cruel is the habit cats have of "playing" with their prey, often for hours, before finally killing it. This is not conscious cruelty. It appears to be an instinctive, inherent characteristic of the domestic cat. According to Muriel Beadle in *The Cat*, it has to do with "readiness" to kill—to follow a neurological pattern.

Even if you do approve of your cat's catching rodents or other prey, you should try to prevent her from eating it. Most well-fed cats will abandon their prey after killing it. If yours doesn't, take it away at once. Wild prey is often infected with various diseases and can also be full of all sorts of internal and external parasites that you don't want your pet to ingest. By praising her lavishly when she brings her catch home you won't discourage your cat from hunting more vermin when you take it away from her.

Getting Stuck in Trees

This is something that seems to happen at least once to almost every young cat who goes outdoors. For one reason or another, she'll find herself up in a tree, higher than she ever intended to go, and the way down looks alarmingly far and steep. She'll immediately start crying piteously until some humans come and stand around the bottom of the tree, wondering what to do.

There are two distinct schools of thought about how to deal with cats in trees. One theory is that if you go away and leave the cat up there, she'll eventually come down by herself; the other is that it's mean to do that, the cat may fall and hurt herself, and you should try to get her down by any means possible.

I've rarely known anyone who was actually able to stick to the former course unless the cat wasn't theirs, or was in a tree so far away from the house that they couldn't hear her sad calls. Although I don't think that cats ever do fall out of trees, most people aren't willing to take that chance, and besides, who can bear to listen to the wailing? In the old days, fire departments sometimes came to the rescue, but I haven't heard of that happening for a long time. Most people seem to have to cope with the problem without the help of a hook and ladder.

I don't remember that Wilbur ever got stuck in a tree, but I'll never forget the time that Francis did. My husband and I had just finished packing to go away early the next morning, and were getting ready to go to bed. While he took the dogs for their bedtime walk,

I usually gave Wilbur and Francis, who was still only four months old, their bedtime snack. On that evening, Wilbur appeared right on cue, but Francis didn't. Going to the back door, I could hear him calling loudly (he has always had an unusually loud voice). When my husband came back, we went out to look for him. We have an awning over the back porch that is about twenty feet off the porch floor and thirty or more feet off the ground. Suddenly Francis's face appeared, upside down over the edge of the awning. He'd apparently climbed up a nearby tree, out onto a branch that hung right over the awning, and gotten stuck there. When we coaxed, he'd go along the length of the branch as far as the tree trunk, but wouldn't attempt to go down the tree. We knew that we couldn't leave him there for the sitter to cope with when we went away, so we had to get him down. The trouble was that our ladder didn't reach from the ground to the branch, and there was no way to get a ladder up from the porch—the awning was in the way. I tried holding up various long poles and sticks, hoping Francis would climb on them, to no avail. My husband tried to climb the tree, but there were no branches at the bottom of the tree to hang on to. It was getting later and later, and we had to get up very early in the morning. Francis kept screaming and running first along the branch and then onto the awning, where he'd hang over the edge looking terrified. All the time, the dogs and Wilbur watched; finally, I said, "For heaven's sake, Wilbur, do something!"

Wilbur looked first at us and then at Francis, who was becoming more and more frantic. He got up slowly and proceeded to climb up the tree. When he reached the branch that Francis was on, he started to "talk" to Francis in a sort of murmur. He backed along the branch, and jumped a short distance to the next lower one. Francis just looked at him, and Wilbur went back up, this time making louder, more insistent noises. He finally got Francis to follow him to the next branch, and then the next, until they were both on the bottom branch, which was still pretty far off the ground. Then Wilbur showed Francis how to climb down the rest of the way, and Francis followed. If we both hadn't seen the whole thing, I don't think that anyone would have believed us! Needless to say, we lavished praise and special treats on Wilbur, but he didn't seem to think that he'd done anything that special. Francis still goes up on the awning once in a while, but he's never gotten stuck again.

As a matter of fact, getting stuck in a high place is almost always a one-time thing for cats: they seem to learn not to go up that high again, or else how to get down if they do, after one incident. If you don't have a Wilbur around to help your young cat out of a tree, the next best thing is to enlist the aid of either a neighborhood youngster who likes cats and is a good tree-climber, or some helpful neighbors and a sturdy ladder.

Fighting

> So they quarrell'd and fit, they scratched
> and they bit.
> —ANON., "The Kilkenny Cats"

Cats fight for two principal reasons: territory and sex. Since your pet cat is undoubtedly neutered, she'll usually fight only if another cat invades her territory. Many pet cats will do almost anything to avoid a fight. When a new cat moved into his neighborhood, Brunswick, a slightly chubby altered male belonging to friends, did everything he could to avoid a confrontation. He hung around a lot on the doorstep. The new-

165

comer was apparently very persistent, venturing far into Brunswick's property. Still Brunswick wouldn't fight, but retreated closer to his house. Our friends could only surmise about the scene that followed, but poor Brunswick got a nasty bite on his rump—not once but three different times in a few months, until the intruder finally either moved away or found someone else to pick on.

There's no more horrifying sound than a real cat fight. When we had cats in the city we never let them go out at night because for quite a few years there were a number of stray cats in the neighborhood. (Unable to get anyone to do anything about them, a lady who lived down the street finally bought a Havahart trap, captured them one by one, and took them to the ASPCA.) Once in a while these cats had terrible fights at night on the back fences. My room was at the back of the house, and their shrieks, moans, and wails used to wake me up and terrify me. I remember that my mother would come into my room in the middle of the night, and we'd open the window and throw pencils at the cats to make them go away—why pencils I don't know, except that they were light and easy to throw, and seemed to do the trick until the next time.

If you hear a cat fight going on nearby, and you suspect that your cat may be involved, it's a good idea to try to stop it. Usually if you turn on an outside light or open a door, the intruder will run away. Cats rarely hurt each other much when they fight unless they're unaltered toms—the sounds of a cat fight are usually much worse than the results. But even small scratches and bites can cause trouble for your cat.

These puncture wounds tend to heal up very quickly. The problem is that they often close up too fast on the surface before they're healed underneath. Then they fester and can turn into abscesses. Most often, cats develop abscesses somewhere on their heads or ears, where there's not much flesh. I was really horrified the first time I saw a cat with an abscess. Jeffrey, who'd been perfectly fine the night before, walked in one morning looking as if he had a gigantic case of the mumps on one side of his face. When an abscess has reached that stage, it has to be opened and drained by a veterinarian.

Early treatment can avoid bad swelling and the need for draining. So even if you don't hear your cat fighting, if she comes in looking as if someone had plucked some fur out or messed it up, especially around the head area, look her over very carefully for small scratches or bites. Clean any wounds, no matter how small, and don't let them scab over too fast. If you notice any swelling, take your pet to the doctor right away so that he can give her antibiotics before the abscess gets bad.

Getting Lost

Unless you let your adult cat out in a strange place, it's virtually impossible for her to get lost. Cats' sense of place is strongly developed. If your cat should disappear, she could be hurt, but more likely she's gotten herself closed in someone's garage or shed.

Brunswick, the cat who was bitten on his rump, once disappeared for several days. His family was frantic; they scoured the neighborhood and looked under every bush, expecting the worst. One day, his young mistress was playing in the back yard when she thought she heard him meowing. Following his cries, she and a friend went through the bushes behind the house into the next-door driveway, where there was a garage. Peering through the window, they saw Brunswick pacing around in the empty garage. With some help, they were able to open the window from the outside and free Brunswick from his prison. He was very hungry and thirsty, but otherwise all right. He must have slipped into the garage when the owners went to get their car out to go away. If the little girls hadn't heard him, he might have still been in there a week later when the owners returned.

We've had cats who disappeared for a rainy night to come home perfectly dry the next day. I'm sure that they were taking shelter in someone's garage, or had found an open window in a cellar. A collar with an indentification tag on it will assure you that your cat will be returned to you if she should turn up in somebody's house. If your cat won't wear a collar, you can have a tattoo put inside her ear—ask your veterinarian about this.

Cars

It's difficult to completely protect your cat from cars if you let her out. Fortunately, most cats stay clear of well-traveled roads, but roads with scant traffic can give a pet a false sense of security. The greatest danger to cats from moving cars is at night. Something seems to happen to cats when they're caught in approaching headlights and they tend either to freeze, or to run in just the direction that a motorist doesn't expect. That's why it's wise to keep your cat in at night. If you can't, a reflecting collar or tag can help a driver spot your pet more easily and determine what direction she's moving in.

Some cat owners have had success in training their cats to stay away from the road by using various unpleasant methods such as throwing gravel or squirting water every time the cat neared the road. I've never found this effective—the cats always seem to think I'm playing with them.

Stationary cars can pose a hazard for cats, too. They often sleep underneath a parked car's engine for warmth, especially in winter. I've known several people who've hurriedly backed out of their driveways only to discover that they've run over their cats. Cats will also sometimes climb right into a car's engine from beneath and can get horribly hurt when the car starts up. Make it a habit to take a quick look underneath your car before starting it, and remind other family members to do so too. Keeping track of your cat and knowing whether she's in or out at a given time can also help to prevent this kind of accident.

Poisoning Outdoors

Cats who go outdoors can be accidentally poisoned. Antifreeze, for example, is very attractive to cats—they seem to find its odor and taste pleasant. It's particularly dangerous, for it takes only about a teaspoon of antifreeze to kill a full-grown cat. Antifreeze evaporates extremely slowly, so don't assume that it will go away by itself. If you use it, or if your car radiator should have a leak, be sure to wash any spills completely away. Check for puddles of antifreeze in drains and gutters and flush them well. Containers that once held antifreeze should be closed tightly before they're thrown away.

Gardeners and other workmen should be warned not to dispose of toxic materials anywhere on your property. We lost Pickles, a six-year-old Siamese, through our own stupidity and a gardener's thoughtlessness. One spring, Pickles seemed "off his feed" and not too well, but I didn't pay a great deal of attention, thinking he'd get better soon. Then one morning, he came crawling into the kitchen moaning loudly, and before we could do anything, he had a violent convulsion. We called the doctor and took him right over to the hospital, where he died less than twelve hours later. An autopsy showed that arsenic poisoning was the cause. We were bewildered until I remembered that the fall before we'd asked a gardener to see if he could rid a flowerbed of slugs. It turned out that without our knowledge he'd doused the earth with arsenic. Apparently now that the ground had thawed, Pickles had been digging holes in the arsenic-saturated flowerbed, licked his paws, and got enough arsenic in his system in the course of several days, or perhaps weeks, to kill him. Of course we felt extremely stupid not to have taken care of him sooner, but it had never occurred to us that the gardener would be foolish enough to use poison near a household with pets and small children. Needless to say, we now make sure that we know exactly what's going on, or in, the earth around our house.

A cat won't usually eat a mouse or rat that has been poisoned, but it's possible for her to catch one and get enough poison on her claws or teeth to be sickened. If you should ever see a stiff or rigid-looking animal lying around, it's probably been poisoned, and you should check your cat carefully to be sure that she hasn't accidentally gotten any poison in her system. The amount of poison a cat can get from catching poisoned prey is usually not enough to do more than make her sick, but she may need some treatment, so observe her carefully.

Emergency Situations

Because the most common emergency situations are accidents of various kinds, I'm including this section here. However, you'll notice that I've also included a few strictly medical emergencies that relate to illnesses described in the previous chapter on health. I won't attempt to cover all of the possible emergency situations you can encounter with your pet, only the most common ones.

All cat injuries and severe illnesses need a doctor's help, but there may be times when you simply can't wait to get to a doctor. Quick action may be necessary in order to save your cat's life, but a panicky reaction can do more harm than good. If your pet is conscious, your calm reassurance can do a great deal to prevent her from becoming excessively frightened and harming herself further.

RECOGNIZING A REAL EMERGENCY

Sudden severe illnesses and accidents can occur in even the best-managed cat households. Your good judgment and calm assessment of the situation can usually determine if there's a true emergency that needs immediate treatment, or if there's time to wait for further observation. Some common feline emergencies requiring really quick action are:

- Known swallowing of poison
- Known traumatic accident such as a severe fall, or being hit by a car, even though there are no obvious injuries
- Choking, or something stuck in the throat
- Unconsciousness

171

- Seeming paralysis
- Prolonged or repeated convulsions
- Severe bleeding
- Sudden pain, characterized by crying out, moaning, panting, trembling
- Inability to breathe or difficulty in breathing
- Inability to urinate; severe pain; bleeding; distention
- Violent vomiting or diarrhea that doesn't stop
- An obvious broken bone
- A severe eye injury
- Snakebite
- Severe allergic reaction to a bee or wasp sting, such as difficult breathing or extreme swelling

EMERGENCY FIRST AID

Before rushing to give aid to a cat, remember that pain, fear, and shock can cause your pet to act irrationally. She may bolt and try to run away and hide, or she may strike out at you in terror. Approach slowly, talking in a soothing voice. Protect your hands and arms, if possible, with gloves and long sleeves, and don't put your face close to an injured or very ill cat. Keep children and everyone else away, except for one reliable helper if you're lucky enough to have one. A lightly tied muzzle (see p. 145) can help you to minister to a very excitable cat, but use one only for a very short period of time.

Have someone call a veterinarian immediately, and follow his instructions as to what to do. If you can't reach a doctor right away, here are some emergency procedures to follow until you can. It might help to remember that the commonsense rules you should follow to treat an injured cat are much the same as standard human first-aid procedures.

172

- Don't ever attempt to give anything by mouth to an injured or very ill cat. Painkillers, tranquilizers, aspirins, and the like can do severe harm and should be administered only under a doctor's orders. Even water can be harmful to an injured or sick cat—she could choke on it.

- If your cat is bleeding, obviously has broken bones, is paralyzed, or if you suspect that she might have internal injuries, *move her as little as possible* and prevent her from trying to move. If you must move an injured cat, don't pick her up in your arms; this could make it hard for her to breathe and might cause further injury. Put her on an improvised stretcher: a cardboard box, window screen, wooden plank, or a large piece of fabric such as a towel, blanket, or even a piece of clothing held taut by several people. Lashing the cat's paws together loosely with a strip of soft fabric will prevent her from struggling too much and trying to jump off the stretcher. A calm helper who can rest a hand lightly on the pet's head or back will help to keep her quiet, too.

- A severe injury or illness can cause a pet cat to go into *shock*. If a cat's paws seem unusually cold, her heartbeat and pulse are alternately rapid and weak, her breath is very shallow and barely audible, and her nose, mouth, and gums appear white instead of pink, you should suspect shock. A sniff of aromatic spirits of ammonia will help to revive her, if you have it handy. It's very important to keep your cat warm with a light covering and get her to a veterinarian at once, as she may need blood or oxygen in order to recover.

- A wound or cut that doesn't stop *bleeding* in about five minutes, or is spurting or bleeding very rapidly, must have immediate attention and can't wait until you can get your pet to a doctor. Pressure applied directly to the wound with a gauze pad, piece of clean fabric, or even your hand will usually cause the bleeding to stop. Several firm wrappings of cloth directly over the wound will staunch the bleeding, but don't leave it bound up tightly for long. If bleeding is very severe, you may need to apply more pressure with your hand. If the bleeding is copious, spurting, and bright-colored, the wound is probably an arterial one, and pressure should be applied between the heart and the wound. Darker blood that flows steadily usually means that a vein is bleeding, and pressure should be below the wound (on the side away from the heart). If you're alone and can't maintain steady pressure while you move your cat, you can use a tourniquet, *but only for very short periods of time*, until you can get help. Any piece of cloth or rope will do, tightened only until the bleeding slows. Applying a tourniquet for a few minutes while you're wrapping the wound with a pressure bandage may help you to be able to work more easily. Use of a tourniquet is *not* advised unless *all* other methods have failed. Severe blood loss will almost always lead to shock, so it's very important to get medical care for your cat as quickly as possible.

- If you think that your pet has a *broken leg*, wrap the injured limb in a rolled-up newspaper or magazine, or make a temporary splint from any firm object (a ruler, for instance) tied on with several pieces of cloth, before attempting to move the animal.

- *Unconsciousness* can be caused by a number of things, among them electric shock, drowning, chok-

174

ing, head injury or other accident, or heart failure. Immediate veterinary diagnosis and treatment is necessary, but artificial respiration and heart massage may keep your cat alive until she gets to the doctor. First check your cat's throat and mouth for foreign objects, mucus, or blood, which might prevent air flow, and clear her breathing passages. Then, cupping one hand under the cat's jaw, place your mouth firmly around her nose, and breathe directly into it. After breathing, remove your mouth so that air can escape, and repeat in a regular rhythm. At the same time, wrap an arm firmly around your cat's chest so that one side of the animal is resting against your body, and your hand is pressing firmly on the other. Press in, firmly, on the chest, and release, repeating regularly at one-second intervals. You can give heart massage in the same way while your cat is lying on her side on a hard surface. Try to get your pet to the doctor at the same time that you're ministering to her. If you detect a pulse or heartbeat, or notice that your pet is starting to breathe by herself, wrap her warmly and rush her to the doctor, continuing your massage if possible.

- If you should come upon your cat with her jaws clamped around a live electric cord, be sure to unplug the cord before touching your pet and treating her for *electric shock*. This may sound like unnecessary advice, but I have heard of people rushing to their pet's aid and getting badly shocked themselves. The shocked cat is probably unconscious and not breathing, so follow the methods prescribed under *Unconsciousness*, above.

- If your cat is *choking* badly, force her mouth open. Using a flashlight if you can, try to locate the offending object. If you can see it readily, you may be able to remove it with your fingertips or a tweezer. If you can't see the object, or are afraid that any attempts to remove it will simply force it farther into your cat's throat, keep her quiet by wrapping her tightly in a towel or blanket, and get her to the doctor.

• *Heat stroke or stress* is usually brought about when a cat is left in a closed car during hot weather, or one parked in the sun even on cool days. Old, fat cats and kittens are particularly likely to be badly affected by extreme heat. A cat with heat stress will act very restless and confused, look dazed, pant a lot, and eventually go into a coma. It's very important to lower the cat's body temperature as quickly as possible. Dunking her in water is the fastest method, but if you can't do that, sprinkle her with water or wrap her in a wet cloth. If you can't get water right away and have some ice cubes, applying them to a cat's forehead and paws will help. At the same time, move her to the coolest spot you can find. Massaging your cat's feet and legs will help to restore her circulation. Oxygen and intravenous fluids are usually needed in order to revive a cat who's been overcome by heat, so your pet should be taken to the doctor as soon as possible.

• Repeated, painful vomiting, accompanied by violent diarrhea, heavy panting, staggering, convulsions, or loss of consciousness are probably signs of *poisoning*. If you know what your pet has ingested, take a sample with you and rush her to the veterinarian at once. If you actually see your pet eat something poisonous, don't wait, but give an emetic right away, *unless* the poison is a corrosive substance, such as acid, alkali, or a petroleum product. Hydrogen peroxide, mixed half-and-half with water, or a strong saline or mustard solution will usually cause your cat to vomit and rid herself of the poison before it can do much harm. After she has vomited, give some raw egg yolk and milk to soothe her stomach. In case of doubt, *don't wait*, but rush your cat to the veterinarian right away. Fast action is essential in the case of poisoning.

- *Convulsions* can be very frightening to watch, but there's nothing that you can, or should, attempt to do to stop one. The best thing that you can do if your cat is having a convulsion is to try to keep her from hurting herself by padding any potentially harmful sharp objects with towels or blankets, and providing a soft landing place if she's off the floor when the convulsion begins. Convulsions are always indications that something's badly amiss in your cat's body, and only a doctor can discover the cause. Taking careful note of the duration of the convulsion, its onset, and other circumstances surrounding it can often help your veterinarian. Try to have someone else accompany you, and wrap your cat firmly in a blanket or towel to protect yourself from bites, and your pet from hurting herself in case she should have another convulsion on the way to the doctor's office.

- A male cat suffering from a *urinary stoppage* is in dire need of immediate veterinary help. (It very rarely occurs in females.) Waste no time trying to minister to him yourself, but get him directly to the nearest doctor or animal hospital. If, however, you can't get to a doctor for more than twenty-four hours, you may want to try to take emergency action. First, feel your cat's bladder. If it's hard, feels like a small rubber ball, and your cat acts as if it hurts when you

177

touch it, then there's probably a stoppage. A greatly enlarged bladder can be ruptured very easily, so use great care. Take your cat's penis in two fingers and roll it very gently between them, working from the body outward, or execute the same motions with a moistened cotton pad. If you're successful, white or slightly bloody gritty material will come out of the tip of the penis, followed by urine. If no urine flows, and you think you've removed all the grit, press on the bladder *very gently* until some urine comes out. Remember, this is only a temporary measure, designed to relieve some of the pressure and prevent possible irreversible bladder or kidney damage. Your cat needs medication and further treatment to recover from a urinary stoppage.

- *Difficult breathing* can be a symptom of *heart failure*. There is little you can do to ease this condition except to keep your pet quiet until she can be treated by a veterinarian. Elevating her head slightly can make breathing easier, and she should be kept warm and completely quiet. Occasionally a cat may have difficult breathing after being *stung* by a wasp or bee. This is an allergic reaction, and the doctor will have to give her a shot to relieve it.

- *Eye irritations* that don't clear up in a day should be treated by a doctor right away to avoid permanent damage. In the meantime, bathing the eye with a piece of cotton saturated with a mixture of baking soda and water will give some temporary relief.

- *Swelling* on the face or ear is usually caused by an *abscess*, which must be thoroughly cleaned and drained in order to heal. Home treatment is possible if you're experienced at it, but a doctor's help is usually needed to prevent further swelling, fever, and infection. Mild swelling can be caused by *insect bites*. If your cat is acting normally otherwise, bathing the bites with cool water will reduce the swelling. But if it is severe or obviously painful, consult the veterinarian.

A FIRST-AID KIT FOR YOUR CAT

Most of the items you'd find in a cat first-aid kit are things that are around in any household. If you're taking your cat from one household to another regularly, or are going to be traveling with your pet, you might want to pack a box with emergency supplies. If you do, here's a general list of things to include:

- A rectal thermometer and Vaseline for lubricating it

- Hydrogen peroxide to clean wounds or abscesses, and to induce vomiting

- Cotton swabs or loose sterilized cotton

- Gauze pads

- Adhesive tape

- Medicine dropper or syringe

- Tongue depressors, or other small wooden pieces for temporary splints

- Blunt-tipped scissors

- Veterinary-supplied or approved ointment for superficial wounds or burns

179

- Aromatic spirits of ammonia as a mild stimulant for the treatment of shock or unconsciousness

- After consulting with your veterinarian, you may want to take some Kaopectate for diarrhea and some mineral oil for constipation. If you're going to an area where it could be needed, include a snakebite kit for your cat (and yourselves).

7

Independent Cat Activities

Commandment II
A Gentleman Cat allows no constraint of
his person, even loving constraint.
—May Sarton, *The Fur Person*

Up until now, I've talked about various aspects of a cat's life in which you're required to take at least some part. The two activities covered in this chapter, sleeping and elimination, are things your cat will do with little, if any, help from you. She'll prefer to be left alone, and will appreciate it if you don't interfere at all, except perhaps to provide the proper facilities when needed, and to see that she has some privacy if your household is a busy one.

Sleeping

How neatly a cat sleeps.
—PABLO NERUDA, ''Cat's Dream''

Cats sleep a great deal. When they're not playing, eating, or washing, they're usually sleeping. Very young and very old cats sleep more than most healthy adults do, but cats who are bored can sleep too much—some

181

for as many as sixteen or more hours out of every twenty-four.

Wherever a cat decides to sleep, she always arranges herself very carefully before settling down. If she's in a cool place, she'll curl up tightly with her tail wrapped around her and her head tucked underneath a paw or leg to retain body heat. If the sleeping place is warm, a cat will often stretch out to her full length, head resting on outstretched front legs; some even sleep on their backs, legs sticking straight up in the air. Sometimes you'll see a cat sleeping in what looks like a very uncomfortable position with her head hanging over the edge of something. This seems to be a favorite position for many cats.

When a cat wakes up, she'll stretch fully, extending her legs out in both front and back, and arching her back and neck. Often she'll then give a mighty yawn, and will frequently wash, especially if she's been resting in a warm place.

KINDS OF CAT SLEEP

> And when you think he's half asleep, he's
> always wide awake.
>
> —T.S. ELIOT,
> "Macavity: The Mystery Cat"

There are apparently two distinct kinds of cat sleep: deep sleep and catnaps.

Like all kinds of animals, cats need to sleep deeply enough to dream for part of every day. During this deep sleep period, cats are very relaxed, and all of the body changes that take place within any sleeping animal occur: lowered blood pressure, slower heartbeat, slower breathing, and so forth. If you watch your cat sleeping, you'll notice that sometimes she'll make small noises, or that her feet will twitch, as if she's trying to chase something. Unless she's disturbing you, don't wake her up—she's simply having a vivid dream. Depending on your cat's usual routine, her deep sleep period can either be at night or during the daytime hours.

Even when cats are deeply asleep, they seem to be able to hear what's going on around them, and can wake up and react quickly if necessary. That's why it's very important that your cat has a quiet, private place where she can go in order to sleep deeply, undisturbed, for part of every day. Children, for instance, should be taught not to disturb sleeping animals.

The other kind of cat sleep, catnapping, is just what it sounds like—a light nap during which a cat's body stays completely ready for action and all of her senses remain alert. Sometimes when a cat naps, it seems as if she's just pretending, and really has one eye open all the time so that she's ready to pounce on anything or anybody coming near. Although a cat who's napping may look at first glance just like a cat in a deep sleep, if you observe carefully you'll notice some differences. For instance, when a cat is simply napping, her breathing stays at the same rate as when she's awake, instead of slowing the way it does when she's deeply asleep. A napping cat will usually open her eyes and look at you if you go close to her or move around the room she's in, no matter how quietly; and if you speak her name softly, she'll stir, or respond in some other way. A deeply sleeping cat generally won't stir unless you insist.

Since a cat's body hasn't undergone any changes when she naps, it won't harm her if she's awakened suddenly. If whatever wakes her is interesting enough, she may abandon her nap completely and join in the activity. If not, she'll simply move away and resume her nap elsewhere.

PLACES FOR CATS TO SLEEP

While cats seem to be able to enjoy a nap in all kinds of unlikely spots, from a two-inch-wide perch on the edge of a bookshelf to a spot in the middle of a noisy room, they're usually more particular about where they settle down for a serious sleep. But even then, the place your cat chooses may seem odd to you.

Cats like a real sleeping place that's warm, quiet, and not too light—away from household traffic and noise. They don't seem to care a bit about softness, and will often choose a hard shelf or table; one cat I knew used to like to sleep in the bottom of an enclosed bathtub when it was still warm from just-drained bathwater. This met another prerequisite for a sleeping place—that it either be off the ground, or else completely free from drafts.

Most cats have several favorite sleeping places that they use interchangeably according to variables such as the weather, household activities, or just whim. As I mentioned in the section on indoor cats, you should try to limit the amount of time that your cat spends sleeping in very hot places such as the top of a radiator or stove. Discouraging her by putting something lumpy or hard on the surface may help, but a really stubborn cat will just sleep on top of whatever you put there to deter her.

On People

> Why at night, small lion, are you so much
> heavier than by day?
>
> —JEAN BURDEN,
> "For a Yellow Cat at Midnight"

Another source of warmth, of course, is another body, either a human's or another pet's. If you have another

184

cat, you may notice that the two pets often curl up together to sleep; even a friendly dog may be a favorite sleeping companion for your cat. Many cats find it best of all to curl up next to you on top of the bedcovers and settle down for a cozy night's rest.

Some owners enjoy having their pet sleep on the bed with them and encourage it, and some cats are better bed companions than others. Pickles, the Siamese, was simply terrible. Every night he'd settle down at the foot of the bed, arranging himself very carefully. Everything was fine until you wanted to turn over or move your feet. Then Pickles would "dig in" and push against you as hard as he could. If you persisted, he'd give your toes a hard nip. When you finally got up in desperation and lifted him off the bed and onto a chair, no sooner would you settle down again than he'd be back! We finally solved the problem by giving him to one of the children to sleep with. (Or the other way around!)

Wilbur, on the other hand, sometimes starts out the night on the foot of the bed, but as soon as he's given the slightest nudge, he gets down and settles somewhere else for the night. A great deal depends on you, and on your cat's sleeping habits.

Cat Beds

> . . . cats show an intense dislike to anything destined or set aside for them.
> —MARGARET BENSON,
> "The Soul of a Cat"

Some cats never seem to care much about shared sleeping quarters and prefer to sleep alone. You can turn one of your cat's favorite nighttime sleeping places into a "bed" for her if you want, by putting a sweater, blanket, or towel on it.

185

You can also purchase, or make, a bed for your cat. A suitable cat bed should have high sides to protect her from drafts, and the bedding should be easy to wash. It's really foolish to buy a cat bed until you're sure that your pet will use it. The best system is to start out with a box or carton that you can line with something soft. You can also cut out one end to make an entrance if you want. If your house is very cold and drafty, covering the box partially with a draped towel will help to keep your cat snug, and will also provide her with the darkness and privacy she craves.

If your pet takes to her makeshift bed, you can eventually replace it with a fancier, bought bed if you wish, placing the new bed in exactly the same place, and using the same liner for a while until she gets used to it. One of the best types of cat bed I've seen is a bean-bag bed. There are several versions on the market—they all are washable, and they form nice high sides around a cat when she sleeps in the center of them. Wicker beds are the least desirable: in addition to being drafty, the porous wicker unfortunately makes a good breeding ground for flea and tick eggs. Moreover, kittens are likely to chew on the beds and swallow bits of wicker.

Some cats will take immediately to any bed you provide, and seem to like the routine of bedtime if you take the time to make a fuss over them. Many won't pay any attention to the bed you choose. If you want to try to teach your pet to sleep in her bed, there are some steps that may help. First and most important, don't ever *put* your cat into a bed. There's a contrary streak in almost all cats that makes them automatically reject anything you insist on—and sleeping is a very private matter. Just leave the bed in a likely spot (preferably one where she already likes to sleep) and let her discover it for herself. Then you can make a great fuss over her the first time you discover her in it. Of course, with a very young kitten, you can start by actually putting her in the bed each night, and she *may* stay there. Placing the bed in a nice warm spot, off the floor, will make it more appealing; if your kitten is really young, you can even line the bed with a well-protected hot-water bottle for the first few nights. *Don't* use a heating pad with any but extremely tiny kittens—older kittens will surely find the wires and chew them. Whatever kind of bed you get, it should be small enough to give your cat a feeling of security and privacy. In addition, a small bed will keep your pet warm on cold nights.

Most owners I know don't see any particular need to fuss about a bed for their cat, and are content to let their pet sleep wherever she wants. The only real advantage to having a bed-trained cat is that, should your pet ever have to stay in a new, strange place, a familiar bed will serve as a good "security blanket," so to speak.

HELPING YOUR CAT CONFORM TO YOUR SLEEPING HOURS

It happens just about every time a new kitten or cat is brought into a household. The owners show her where they'd like her to sleep, go to bed themselves, and turn off the light. It can be just as soon as the light's off, or later on as they're finally falling into a deep sleep. Suddenly something gallops across the bed, thunders off, and returns again to leap up one side of the bed and down the other. (For some reason, even the daintiest kitten can be very heavy-footed in the middle of the night.) In another version, if the bedroom door is closed, the new owners are awakened by a terrible crash, or series of crashes, coming from

187

somewhere in the house. Sometimes a cat's frantic nighttime activity is accompanied by loud howls.

After the amazement has worn off, you may decide that the best course of action is to close your new cat up somewhere for the remainder of the night so that you can get some sleep. Very often, this just makes her more frantic, and the result is that you're kept awake by the cat's loud and very pitiful-sounding cries and wails of protest: she may even hurl herself against the door repeatedly.

What you need to bear in mind is that because cats are nocturnal animals, they're naturally wakeful at night until they adapt to a new schedule. If your new cat hasn't lived in a household before, she's probably never slept through the night, and has no idea what's expected of her. Even if she has been living in a home, she's undoubtedly been with a bunch of other cats or kittens until now and not only is lonely, but hasn't used up sufficient energy alone in a house with you all day to be tired enough to sleep. Strangeness, loneliness, and confusion can all combine to make your new cat restless, edgy, and wakeful. Her hysterical reaction is a rather pointed request for your help.

What can you do to help your new cat feel secure enough to calm down? Scolding will do no good, because your pet won't have a clue what in the world you're scolding her for—it's likely to confuse her more. If you're not averse to having a cat sleep on the bed with you, hold your pet close and stroke her gently. This will usually calm her down right away, make her feel secure, relaxed, and warm, and put her to sleep. If you don't want your cat on your bed, the warmth of a cozy nest placed near you may help her to sleep. Kittens almost always sleep after eating, so a snack may help, too.

The next day, be sure that your new kitten gets

plenty of exercise. A vigorous rough-and-tumble game or a session of fetch or chase just before bedtime should tire her out. If you're at home during the day, try to keep your new pet busy and active so that she doesn't sleep for too long. Contrary to my advice above about not interrupting a cat's deep sleep, don't allow your new pet to sleep for too long in the daytime until she gets into the routine of sleeping deeply at night. Give her something to eat at bedtime, and take the time to stroke and pet her. If you want her to learn to sleep in her own bed, encourage her to get in it (remember, don't put her in—she'll just get out until she accepts the bed), and praise her if she does.

It usually takes only one or two nights for your new kitten or cat to adapt to your sleeping routines. Problems can arise, however, if nobody's home at all during the day. Your pet will naturally sleep most of the time and be raring to go at night. If extra-long playtimes, a lot of attention and bedtime petting, and a snack don't solve the problem, discuss the situation with your veterinarian. He may have some suggestions about diet or exercise that can help. Sometimes another kitten to play with can be the answer, but remember that that could lead to having four pairs of feet running across your stomach all night, so don't assume it's a foolproof solution!

Bathroom Habits

> The cat is never vulgar.
> —CARL VAN VECHTEN,
> *A Tiger in the House*

Cats have a well-deserved reputation for being clean animals. From the time kittens are born until they learn

189

to walk, they're kept clean by their mother, who frequently licks each kitten's genital and anal area to stimulate elimination and then washes the resulting urine and feces off. As soon as a kitten learns to walk well, at about three to four weeks, the mother cat shows her where to relieve herself: as often as necessary, she'll take each kitten, carry her to the spot she wants her to use (in most households that's a litter tray), and demonstrate how to proceed. If left to her own devices, the mother will choose to take the kittens for elimination to a spot some distance from their sleeping area so that odor won't attract would-be predators. For the same reason, cats always carefully bury their waste (except during mating rituals, when the object is to establish territorial rights and possibly attract a mate).

There can be exceptions to this well-ordered routine. Some mother cats seem to lose interest in their kittens once they're old enough to leave the nest, and neglect the all-important step of showing them where to "go" now. This occurs most commonly when the mother is extremely young, or if she has had too many litters too close together. It can also happen when the mother comes into heat again while the kittens are still very young (it's possible for this to happen only ten to fourteen days after delivery), and her primary concern becomes finding another mate. A very dirty litter pan or one which is used by other cats may keep a mother cat from putting her kittens in it, too. In rare cases, there can be a mother who was never taught properly herself and thus won't know enough to train her kittens. Of course, if a kitten is brought up with nothing but a hard surface and no available litter (for example, in a cage of some sort), she'll learn, perforce, to "go" anywhere at all.

This is one more good reason for you to try to observe your potential new pet at home with her mother. Be suspicious if you notice that a kitten hasn't used the litter tray, or if the tray is excessively dirty or smelly. If a kitten or cat is in a cage and there's no litter tray in sight, ask about it—it's possible that the tray was just removed for cleaning, but perhaps the cat has never been trained to use one. While it's certainly possible for a young kitten or cat to make a "mistake" and miss the tray by a few inches, you should be wary if there's evidence of a lot of errors. You *can* teach a young, untrained cat to use a litter tray, but it may be a difficult process, so why get yourself into it if you can avoid it?

Even if you plan to let your cat go outdoors regularly, you should still provide her with a readily accessible litter tray somewhere in the house. You won't be allowing your new pet outside, anyway, until she's either old enough or at home enough not to go away or get into trouble, so you'll need a litter tray in any event. There are several reasons why you ought to maintain a litter tray even for a cat who usually uses the outdoors. She'll need it if the weather's particularly inclement; if you go out and leave her closed in the house for a long time; or if she's not feeling too well. There can also be times when you don't want her to go out at all for a while—if she's been ill, or is on medication, for instance. If you need to check on the condition of your cat's urine or feces, or to take a sample to the doctor, it will be much easier all around if she's already used to using a litter tray occasionally.

LITTER TRAYS

Once you've decided that you're going to get a cat, the first thing that you should purchase is the litter tray, which should be filled and ready for use when you bring your new pet home. Nerves and excitement can often create some urgency in a new cat's insides, and it's very important to start her off right from the beginning. If possible, the litter tray should be placed in the spot where it's going to remain—cats are habitual creatures. If this isn't practical for some reason—if, for instance, you're starting your new pet off in a small room and will eventually let her have the run of the house—be sure that you always show her exactly where the tray is. If you have a large house or apartment, two or more litter trays may be a good idea, particularly if your cat is very young or old, and can't wait too long. All cats need to know that there will be a clean litter tray in a regular, customary place that is private and quiet.

The litter tray itself should be made of material that is easy to wash: baked enamel or plastic is best. It should be about two feet long by one and a half feet wide, and the sides need to be high—four or five inches at least. Most cats cover their waste very vigorously, and if the sides of the tray aren't high enough, some litter will be kicked out. A plastic tray or newspapers placed under the tray will make cleanup easier and also protect the floor if your cat should miss slightly. There are litter trays made with snugly fitted removable covers equipped with an entrance hole; they protect a cat's privacy, and a good side benefit is that they contain most flying litter. If you have a very tiny kitten, she may not be able to negotiate a high-sided litter tray for a while. A practical solution to this problem is to use a low-sided cardboard box well-lined with plastic. Your kitten won't produce a great volume of waste while she's small, and by the time she does, she'll be able to graduate to a larger, regular tray.

The litter tray should be lined either with layers of newspaper or with plastic liners, available in pet-supply stores. By lining the tray, you can remove the entire contents by simply lifting the whole thing by the edges. Litter material must be at least two inches deep so that your cat can dig a hole in it. Cats usually like to use the same kind of litter material that they've become accustomed to; if you want to change later on, you can do so gradually by adding the new material to the old in increasing proportions, but for the moment, it's best to stick to whatever your new cat has been using. If your pet has been going outside, mix some earth with the litter for a while.

There are a number of commercial litter materials for sale. Clay litter is often best because it absorbs odors and moisture readily, doesn't stick to a cat's fur, and, if some is swallowed, will do no harm. There are some cats, however, who get a cough from breathing the considerable dust created by clay litter. If this dust disturbs either you or your pet, try the green variety of litter. This is much more expensive, but it does absorb odors better than the plain kind, and it doesn't create a cloud of dust when it's poured or dug in. Some cats seem to dislike the green litter intensely, so be sure to test a small bag. Some breeders and owners use other litter-tray fillers such as sawdust, peat moss, sand, earth, or shredded newspaper. All of these materials are all right in an emergency, but they either don't absorb and deodorize well, or are too easily tracked around on a cat's feet and aren't very satisfactory for home use. A layer of plain baking soda spread in the bottom of the tray before adding litter will help absorb odors better than most commercial "cover-ups."

You and your cat will have to work out your own schedule for litter-tray–cleaning, but a good rule of thumb is to remove all solid matter at least once a day with a slotted spoon, sieve, or spatula made expressly for this purpose (clay litter, by the way, makes this easy and neat to do, since it completely coats solid matter, and can be flushed down the toilet). Change the entire tray at least once a week. If more than one cat uses the tray, it starts to smell or look damp, or your cat lets you know that she's not happy with its condition, you should change it more often. After the litter and liner have been removed, the tray should be washed in hot soapy water and dried thoroughly before refilling. Smelly disinfectants may cling to the tray, especially if it's made of plastic, and don't usually need to be used. Be sure to wear gloves, or wash your hands thoroughly after handling a cat's litter tray or removing droppings to prevent possible contact with toxoplasma.

OTHER PLACES

It's possible to teach your cat to use the toilet bowl instead of a litter tray if you want to. Years ago, I knew a Siamese whose owners taught her this "trick": first they placed her litter tray on top of the lid of a closed toilet; then when she was used to that they put a shallow tray with a small amount of litter in it underneath the rim of the seat; and eventually they removed the tray altogether. There are now commercially manufactured "kits" that come with instructions for training a cat to use the toilet. I recently saw a device on television that enables a cat to flush after using the toilet by touching a specially wired button with her paw, thus eliminating one possible objection to toilet-using by cats! (I don't think that this is on the market yet.) I've never tried this system, but it seems like a good idea, doing away with the odor, mess, and expense of litter. I'm not sure that all cats will take to it, but if you think it would work well for you and your cat and you have the time and patience, try it, but don't ever forget to leave the lid up.

If you plan to let your cat go out, you'll probably prefer that she use the outdoors as a general rule instead of her litter tray. Most cats get the idea right away, and soon establish regular outdoor places to go—usually in the soft earth of a flowerbed, or in the shelter of some bushes or branches.

Some cats don't seem to want to use the earth. No matter how much time they spend outdoors they'll always come in to use their litter trays. If you'd like to teach your reluctant cat to "go" outdoors, you can try placing her tray in a likely protected spot and showing it to her. Usually she'll get the hint after a few times, but she still may prefer to use her indoor tray a good deal, and you'll probably just have to accept her decision.

WHY DOES A CAT BREAK TRAINING?

There are a number of possible reasons why a formerly well-trained cat will suddenly break training and start to use all sorts of strange places as a bathroom instead of her litter tray. Some favorite "secret" places for cats to use are: underneath or behind a heavy, skirted piece of furniture; in fireplace ashes; in the bathtub; in planters or large plant pots; somewhere in a damp corner of a cellar or crawl space; anywhere that's not frequented often by people, such as the attic or a rarely used room.

If you don't provide a litter tray for your indoor-outdoor cat, she may be forced to find somewhere in the house to use in emergencies. This winter, I discovered that Wilbur was urinating in the bathtub. He was so neat, aiming directly down the drain, that I never would have known about it if I hadn't seen him one day. He was very embarrassed, and I felt bad because I'd recently decided that it wasn't necessary to have a litter tray in the house anymore.

An entirely indoor cat who has a readily available litter tray often makes mistakes because she wasn't trained right in the first place. Her mother may have done a poor job of teaching her, or you may have given her too much freedom at first, before she became used to using a litter tray. It's very possible not to notice when a young kitten goes outside her tray. Small kittens don't have much waste, and there's virtually no odor at all to their urine and very little to their feces if they're healthy. If more than one cat is using the same litter tray, it's often very hard to keep track of a young kitten's frequency of elimination. It's not until a cat starts to approach sexual maturity at about six months that owners become aware of the problem because of the odor, and think that the cat has suddenly broken training, when in fact she hasn't been trained all along. The only solution to this problem is to set about training your cat properly.

When a formerly well-trained adult cat breaks training it's a different matter. A clean cat usually won't abandon her litter tray unless she's under a great deal of stress. She'll be just as upset about it as you are, and scolding her will only compound the whole thing. You can usually figure out what the problem is by careful observation. Most often, a cat will break training for three general reasons: there's something physically wrong with her; there's something emotionally or psychologically amiss; or there's something the matter with the facilities you're providing for her to use. Once you've diagnosed the cause of your cat's sudden misbehavior and remedied it, she'll probably go right back to using her litter tray all the time. If not, you'll need to give her some help.

Physical Problems

Illness is the most common reason why a well-trained cat breaks training suddenly. Severe diarrhea, which can be caused by sickness or worms, can create dire emergencies that can't wait, and your pet may have to "go" anywhere at all. Bladder or kidney infections, cystitis, or other urinary-tract problems can also create a sense of urgency your cat can't ignore. While diarrhea will be pretty obvious, frequent urination may not be as readily noticed right away, especially if each time your cat wets only a little bit. You should suspect something's wrong if your cat's litter tray doesn't seem to be as damp as usual.

Another problem that can confront a young or very old cat is being accidentally shut away from her pan. While a healthy adult may be able to hold on until someone comes home or notices that the wrong door is closed, youngsters and senior citizens often don't have the physical ability to wait very long. If this happens frequently, you may have to relocate the litter tray, or put another one somewhere else.

Unneutered cats also have a physical characteristic that often precludes the use of a litter tray. Females in heat not only cry continually, but, if they're closed in the house, may also urinate frequently in various places in an effort to attract a mate. Tomcats are even more difficult to house-train, even when they're allowed outdoors some of the time. During the mating season, which lasts from six to eight months each year, tomcats have a very strong sense of territory, even when there's no female around. They mark off their territory by backing up to a stationary object, such as a wall, tree, or piece of furniture, raising their tails, and spraying their strong-smelling urine just at cat-nose-level. (A cat's tail during urination usually sticks straight out behind, parallel to the ground.) Male cats spray often, leaving a small amount in many places. Occasionally there are unaltered males who don't display this behavior for years, and then suddenly do so when a female or another tom moves into the area; owners mistakenly think that their pet is suddenly breaking training, when in fact he's acting perfectly natural for a tomcat.

Emotional or Psychological Problems

An interesting variation of sexual spraying is when an altered male suddenly starts to spray. Usually a well-trained altered cat will confine this uncharacteristic activity to the outdoors, but an indoor cat may suddenly startle his owners by spraying in his pan. The reason is usually that a tomcat is threatening your altered male's territory, and even though he doesn't always react sexually, this instinctive behavior will suddenly surface. Recently, I was very surprised to see Wilbur back up to a bush in the front of our house and spray—as far as I know he's never sprayed before in the nine years we've had him. The next day I noticed that a young tom had moved in two doors away, and Wilbur had obviously been marking off his territory as a warning to the newcomer. This probably won't occur unless your cat goes outdoors, but if your indoor altered male should suddenly start to spray in the house, you can protect the wall behind his pan temporarily with a piece of plastic, and suggest to the owners of the tom that they either have him altered, or keep him at home. (It will probably not do much good, but it's worth a try.) With altered males, the instinct usually isn't very strong, and your disapproval will probably lead him to stop.

A change in the household can also cause a cat suddenly to break training, as a form of protest or an outgrowth of jealousy. A new pet who's getting a lot of attention may put your old cat's nose out of joint, and she may decide to get some notice by breaking training. A new baby may have the same effect, especially if your cat has been the "baby" up till now. So can the loss of a favorite human, especially if it's the person who paid the most attention to the cat. If you're aware of the situation, you can usually remedy it by giving your pet a lot of affection, seeing to it that she has your undivided attention for a while each day, and generally assuring her that she hasn't been forgotten.

Stress is another reason why a formerly well-trained cat may stop using her litter tray. A cat who's always lived in a relatively calm household may not be able to handle a sudden influx of children or noisy houseguests, and will often react by forgetting her training. Usually when she's provided with a quiet place to retreat to and becomes used to the confusion, she'll go back to her former training.

Moving, work being done in the house, or other upheavals can also cause your cat to become confused about using her litter tray. Sometimes cats who don't know what else to do will use their beds if they have them—clearly this is due to temporary confusion or upset. If you're able to anticipate the problem, accustom your pet to staying in a closed room with her litter tray for part of each day while the work is going on.

Problems with the Facilities

Something about the tray you've provided or its location may cause your pet suddenly to decide that she can't use it anymore. A dirty tray is often the problem. If you've been busy and forgotten to clean the tray, your pet may not want to get in it. Use of the same tray by a recently acquired second cat may be distasteful to your pet, and will also necessitate more frequent tray cleaning.

Most cats heartily dislike the smell of disinfectants and deodorants. If you've changed brands, it's possible that the odor may be too strong; or perhaps you didn't rinse the tray thoroughly enough. Plastic litter trays will eventually absorb the smell of disinfectants and should be replaced. Even if you can't detect any smell yourself, remember that your cat's sense of smell is very strong, and she may not be using her tray anymore because it smells terrible to her.

Your cat may not like the kind of litter you're providing, and will refuse to use it. Don't change brands, or types, of litter abruptly—always try to mix some of the old kind with the new until your pet becomes used to it.

A tray location that may have been fine in the past can become unsatisfactory with a change in household routines. Cats like some privacy and quiet for litter-tray activities, and if the spot that the tray is in has suddenly become a major walk-through or gathering place, it won't do anymore. A cat who is suddenly faced with lots of company or frequent interruptions when she's using her pan will find somewhere else to go that's less public.

RETRAINING A CAT WHO'S BROKEN TRAINING

The first thing to do is to determine the cause of your cat's misbehavior. Once you've discovered the cause and corrected it, you may still have to help your pet to relearn to use her tray.

If you decide that your cat was probably never properly trained in the first place, you'll need to start from scratch, by providing her with a roomy, clean litter tray and closing her in the room with it when you're not around to watch her. If she doesn't seem to understand what the tray is for, put her in it and show her how to dig in the litter by taking her front paw and making digging motions with it. If you're around, place your cat in her litter tray immediately after she eats, and when she first wakes up—cats often "go" then, and this may help her to get the idea. Unless she has been raised in a cage with no litter, she'll prefer to use litter rather than a hard surface, so a tiled room is the best place to train her in. Once she gets the idea and uses the tray on her own, you should praise her lavishly. If the tray is roomy, clean, and in a sufficiently private place, most cats will learn in a very short time. But, until you're sure that you can trust your pet, don't let her out of your sight when she's loose in the house, or you may have to start all over again. If she should start to "dig" in the corner of the living room, pick her up immediately, scold her, and put her in her tray.

In order to prevent a cat who's broken training from continuing in her bad habits even after their cause is remedied, you'll have to eradicate all traces of odor from her former mistakes, or your pet will probably use the same spots again. This can be difficult, because urine odors in particular permeate upholstered furniture and carpets and are hard to remove. A good professional cleaning will get rid of the odors, but if this isn't practical, a mixture of vinegar and water applied after the spot has been thoroughly washed will often do the trick. Strong-smelling disinfectants and commercial products designed specifically to mask urine odors probably work, but they may also drive you out of your house with their own offensive odors.

Some people advocate sprinkling red pepper or scattering mothballs around the areas you want your cat to avoid, but I've seen many cats calmly walk right into the middle of areas treated with these substances.

You'll also have to make it hard for her to use other favorite spots. If your cat's been "going" in the fireplace, remove all the ashes after every fire and get a snug screen. If she likes your planter or a large flowerpot, cut a piece of screen or chicken wire to fit around the plant stems and cover the earth with it. It may not look too great, but it will save your plants from certain death. Leaving an inch or two of water in the bottom of the bathtub or shower stall will discourage your cat from using these areas as a toilet, and keeping closet, attic, and cellar doors closed will keep her from going back to these places when you're not looking.

Providing more than one litter tray can often help, too. Laziness, forgetfulness, or urgency can make it hard for an older cat to wait too long, and a handy litter tray will make it more convenient for her. If you find that you can't trust your cat entirely despite all your efforts, it's best to close her in a room with a litter tray when you go out—it makes it easier for both of you.

SECTION THREE

Coping with Some Other Aspects of Cat Care

Cats are not at all like people
Cats are Cats.
—WILLIAM JAY SMITH, "Cat"

8

Cats and Places

But the cat came back
For it wouldn't stay away.
—ANON., "The Cat Came Back"

Cats' strong territorial instinct is well documented. Their built-in sense of property can sometimes cause problems. Just as it's very difficult to prevent a cat from violating man-made boundaries and wandering into a neighbor's yard, it can also be hard to transplant an adult cat to completely new territory.

Owners are often annoyed when a pet cat acts frightened and upset in a strange location despite their efforts at reassurance, and nothing can be more frustrating or irritating than trying to cope with what seems to be an irrationally terrified animal. But if you can learn to understand and accept your cat's feelings about places, you can probably do a lot to help make physical transitions easier for her. At least you'll be better equipped to make intelligent decisions about whether it's wise to uproot your cat at all.

Strong Attachments to Places

It's currently popular to debunk the "incredible-journey" stories about cats that proliferated a while ago. One well-known animal behaviorist recently told a story about himself demonstrating that he'd been mistaken about the return of his long-lost cat, and in reality had taken in a look-alike.

I used to take all of the miraculous-return tales with a grain of salt, too, until I actually witnessed one. Friends of ours who live way out in the country had a pair of young part-Siamese brothers named Spic and Span. The cats were very handsome, bright, and lively. The only problem was that our friends couldn't get them to stop catching every bird, chipmunk, and baby rabbit in sight. No matter what they did, Spic and Span continued to decimate the wildlife on their property. Finally, our friends decided they couldn't keep the cats anymore and found a good home for them about twenty miles away.

The new owners were delighted with the cats, and decided that it was a good idea to keep them indoors for a while until they became used to their new home. All seemed fine, and Spic and Span apparently settled down quite contentedly. After about a month, the new owners decided that it was safe to allow the cats to have some freedom. No sooner was the door opened, however, than Spic and Span took off like streaks across the yard and into some adjacent woods. The new owners searched and called to no avail. Finally, they sadly called our friends to report what had happened.

Two weeks later, Spic appeared on our friends' doorstep. He was thin but unharmed. Strangely, there was no sign of Span. After several weeks went by, everyone assumed that something had happened to

Span and that he wouldn't be returning. On Thanksgiving Day, three and a half months after Spic's reappearance, we were all sitting at the dinner table at our friends' house in midafternoon. Suddenly Spic jumped up from the floor where he'd been napping and flung himself at the front door, calling loudly. Puzzled, someone got up and opened the door, and there was Span, bounding across the front lawn toward the house! There was a somewhat frantic reunion, the cats sniffing, licking, rubbing, and purring, while the people stood around in amazement. Span seemed well fed and in good health, and the only explanation that we could come up with was that somebody had caught him and kept him closed up for four months. As soon as he could, Span had escaped and made a beeline home again. Our friends decided that if Spic and Span had gone to all that trouble getting back to them, they'd better keep them despite their hunting.

The interesting thing to me about Spic and Span's return was that they'd always seemed more devoted to each other than to their owners. Since they'd been together in their new home, it seemed pretty clear that the main reason for their twenty-mile odyssey was a wish to return to what they considered to be their territory.

Helping Your Cat Adjust to New Places

> Observe a cat entering a room for the first time: it searches and smells about, it is not quiet for a moment, it trusts nothing until it has examined and made acquaintance with everything.
> —JEAN-JACQUES ROUSSEAU,
>   "Observe a Cat"

207

Even though many cats become strongly attached to places that they consider to be their territory and resist any move, there are also plenty of cats who do travel with their owners without seeming to have any qualms about it. Jeffrey, for instance, went away with us a lot and didn't seem to mind; he adjusted so well, in fact, that he never wanted to go home. Many owners regularly take their pet cats with them for weekends and summers away: I know a couple whose young cat enjoys camping trips with them, in a different spot each time.

Owners with cat-travel experience know that it's very important to pack carefully for their pets, even for short trips. Familiar bedding, toys, dishes, and an ample supply of your pet's regular food will help her to feel more secure no matter where you take her.

SHORT VISITS

If you plan to have your cat accompany you on frequent visits, accustom her to short stays when she's still young. You can take her for hour-long visits to a nearby friend's house for practice. By becoming used to going to a new place and then returning home, your cat will realize that nothing bad will happen to her, and that you're not going to desert her or leave her behind in a new place.

When a cat arrives in an unfamiliar place, she'll always explore every nook and cranny carefully before settling down. As soon as you get to your destination, open the carrier. Cats often like to sit in their carrying cases for a while, looking around and sniffing the air before getting out. Don't rush your pet; let her take her time deciding to leave her familiar carrier. Snatching her out and putting her down in a strange room too quickly can frighten her. When she does decide to venture out, pat and reassure her and then leave her alone for a while to get used to her new surroundings. If you hover too much, you'll give your pet the idea that there's something to be nervous about. Leave some water handy, and be sure to show your cat her litter tray before you go away. Don't attempt to feed your pet too soon after you arrive in a new place—let her stomach calm down first.

If you're in a strange house, it's a good idea to confine your cat to one room or a closed area for a while, or for the entire visit if it's a short one. If you can tolerate her with you at night, the best place to keep your cat is in your bedroom. A cat who's not used to closed doors will probably protest when you leave her shut in. Nevertheless, it's safest to confine your pet until you're sure that she won't panic and hide in some inaccessible place, or escape through an open door or window and run off.

When you're staying in a hotel or motel, be sure to leave a Do Not Disturb sign on the door if you go out and leave your cat in the room. Or close your pet in the bathroom with a clearly lettered No Entry notice on the door. Many cat owners leave their pets in their carrying cases when they have to be away from the room for a short time. Most cats will settle down and go to sleep. If you'll be staying in hotels a lot with your cat and you travel by car, you may want to buy a cat cage. Once your pet gets used to sleeping in her cage it will keep her safe and give her more room to move around in than a carrier will.

LONGER STAYS AND MOVING

Even when you take your cat away for a long stay, let her become accustomed to her new surroundings a little at a time. If you're going to be in one place for the whole summer, for instance, it's best to keep your pet in one room or small area until the strangeness wears off and she gets used to the sounds and smells of her temporary new home.

We learned this the hard way once when we took Pong, the Siamese we had when I was growing up, away for the summer. We'd rented a house at the beach, and Pong had been there with us several years before, so we anticipated no problems with him. When we arrived after a long drive, Pong was screaming loudly in his carrier as he always did throughout any trip. We took the carrier inside and opened up the lid, thinking he'd be delighted to get out. After a moment's pause, he jumped out of the carrier and started to slink around the room. As he reached the front door, my father walked in with some bags. Pong scooted out the door and before anyone could catch him, he ran under the front porch, behind some lattice-work, and squeezed back as far as he could possibly go. He sat there hunched up, and no efforts at cajoling him out worked. Finally, we decided to leave him alone, thinking he'd come out later on. Two days later he was still there—he apparently came just far enough when nobody was around to drink the water we left for him, but as soon as anyone went near, he'd scrunch even farther back into his hiding place. Short of taking the porch apart there was nothing we could do, so we kept replenishing the water and waited. After five days, we were sitting on the porch one evening when we heard Pong's typical Siamese yowls of "Let me in." He strolled into the house, went straight to the kitchen, where he ate heartily, and then settled down on a chair near us and went to sleep. From then on he seemed perfectly at home in the beach house. When we went back home in the fall, we were very careful to keep him closed in my bedroom until he remembered where he was and settled down.

You'll want to make the whole process as easy for your cat as you can if you have to move. Moving to a new home probably won't be as traumatic for your cat as a visit to a strange place, because familiar furnishings and objects will be around. Even if you plan to get all new furniture or have everything redone, try to keep one of your cat's favorite chairs intact for a while to help her feel more at home. Again, let her get to know the new house gradually, and be very careful to keep your pet safely closed in if you're having any work done. The combination of a new home, the noise of work, strange people around, and an open door can make escape seem very desirable to any cat. Many moving companies, by the way, have prepared pamphlets with hints on how to move a pet that are available for the asking.

Even if your cat is very independent and used to going outdoors, you'll have to be very careful about letting her out alone in a new place for a while. She just may think that she can get "home" easily. When we moved two blocks away from our old house, Oliver and Pickles turned up on our former doorstep several times until it finally sank in that we weren't there anymore. If your move is in the same neighborhood, alert the new owners of your old house about your cat so that they can keep an eye out for her and call you if she shows up. Be especially sure that your cat wears identification all the time in case she gets lost trying to get "home."

If you move far from your old home, it's a good idea to keep your cat inside for a week or more until you're sure that she's accepted the new house and settled down. The first few times you let her out, go with her and talk to her to remind her that you're there. When you first let her out alone, keep an eye on her, and try not to let her stay out for very long, especially at night. Other cats can present a problem for a newcomer, and your cat may have to stand up for her rights a few times. Be sure to check her over for wounds if you think she's been fighting.

Once your cat has established new favorite sleeping areas, explored every inch of the entire house and yard, and settled things with the cat neighbors, she'll usually accept your decision to move and settle down happily in her new home.

Traveling with a Cat

> Cats are extremely nervous and they are not as a rule to be trusted in railroad trains—fast moving objects usually inspire them with the keenest sense of fright.
>
> —CARL VAN VECHTEN,
> *A Tiger in the House*

Cats vary a great deal in their reaction to travel. Many cats these days seem to be unfazed by frequent trips. Some show cats, for instance, make numerous cross-country trips each year with no apparent ill effects. The average pet cat, however, can be very unnerved by being bumped around in a speeding vehicle assailed by strange and terrifying noises and odors, while she's closed in her carrying case.

If you know that you'll be taking your cat on many trips, you can help her to be a better traveler by starting to get her used to it when she's young. Give frequent "refresher" courses until your cat's fully grown; otherwise, if several months go by between trips, a young cat is likely to forget not to be afraid, and you'll

212

have to start all over again. As a cat gets older, her good memory can serve as either a help or a hindrance to travel—while good early conditioning can turn your pet into a lifelong good traveler, one bad experience can sour her on it forever.

In addition to conditioning your cat to travel, there are several other things that you should do before taking her on a long trip. It's important that she be in good health— ailments that seem minor at home can turn into major problems when you're far away from your own doctor. While you're at the veterinarian's having your cat checked over, make sure that her immunizations are completely up to date. Many states and all foreign countries require a signed health and/or vaccination certificate for nonresident animals. Your veterinarian will also know if there are any particular health regulations or problems in the areas you plan to visit; your cat may need additional immunizations in some places.

Even if your cat is a good traveler, you should have your veterinarian prescribe a tranquilizer in case she becomes upset. Test the medication out at home before you leave for efficacy and possible side effects. (Note: Never give a cat tranquilizers intended for people or other pets—the dosage is very exact.)

If you're planning on leaving the United States with your cat, you'll need to know the entry and departure regulations for the countries you'll be visiting, and the United States requirements for returning. The ASPCA in New York City has an up-to-date booklet for sale that contains travel and immunization regulations for travel to every state in the Union and 110 foreign countries, in addition to a number of other useful travel tips for pets.*

Be sure to remember to pack for your cat as care-

*For information, write to the American Society for the Prevention of Cruelty to Animals, Education Department, 441 East Ninety-second Street, New York, NY 10028.

fully as you do for yourself. In addition to familiar objects and dishes, take along an ample supply of medication and food from home if it's not readily available where you're going. A change in diet is sure to upset a traveling cat. If you're going with your pet, carry along a thermos of water from home—this will also help to prevent digestive upsets while you're en route. Some flea powder and spray will be helpful if you're traveling during warm weather or going to a warm climate. Dusting your cat with powder lightly each day and spraying hotel or motel rooms on arrival will prevent your pet from picking up any fleas left behind by former animal visitors.

If you're planning to stay in hotels or motels along the way with your pet, make sure that she'll be accepted beforehand. Many hostelries will gladly accept well-behaved cats, especially if you point out that your pet will sleep in her carrier or cage, but they often have certain limited areas set aside for people with pets, so it's wise to phone ahead to reserve a room.

GOING BY CAR

A majority of cats will travel quite well in a car if they ride in a carrying case they've become used to. Most will protest in the beginning, but once you're under way, the motion of the car usually puts a cat right to sleep. (There are exceptions, like Pong, who scream for the entire trip.) As I said before, if you anticipate many car trips with your cat, get her used to the smell, motion, and noise early in her life. A good way to do this is to put your pet in her carrier every few days and drive around the block several times. Just remember that you'll have to repeat this routine at frequent intervals if you want your young cat to continue to accept car travel as she gets older.

Don't feed your cat for at least four hours before going on a car trip. If she tends to be very nervous or has a particularly sensitive stomach, allow more time. While some cats do suffer from actual motion sickness, most veterinarians agree that when a cat vomits during a car ride, it's usually a sign of nerves. If your cat continually gets sick to her stomach during car trips, even on an empty stomach, a mild tranquilizer will probably help.

Some cats have been so traumatized by a scary car trip that they never recover sufficiently to ride calmly; others are so high-strung that they can't adjust to travel. If your pet is terribly upset and frightened in the car, you'll probably want to sedate her. Usually a tranquilized cat will go right to sleep in her carrier and will arrive at her destination in a slightly dopey but relaxed state.

Be sure to take along plenty of fresh water and a bowl so that you can offer your cat a drink at each stop. This is important even in cool weather, because anxiety can make a cat very thirsty. A small litter tray that she can use in the car is also essential equipment—plastic liners will make it easy to dispose of the contents along the way. Again, offer your cat the use of the tray at every stop.

Be absolutely sure that your cat is securely leashed before you open a car door or window when you stop. Holding her is not a good idea. If she panics she'll dig her claws into you and you'll probably drop her. The best system is to leave a harness on your cat while she's riding in her carrier so that you can snap a leash on the minute you open the lid. Don't leave a leash on you cat while she's in the carrying case, however; it's too easy for her to become tangled in it.

Never leave your pet in a closed car if you can possibly avoid it. Even during cool weather the "green-

215

house effect'' of the sun on glass and metal can make the interior temperature of a car reach dangerous heights very fast. With car windows open, it takes less than five minutes for the sun to make the temperature inside a car climb to 120 degrees on a typical summer day. If you *must* leave your cat in the car at all, be sure to park in the shade and check every ten minutes to be sure that the sun hasn't shifted. Offer your cat a cool drink before you leave her. You should also be aware of the possibility that your cat might be stolen if she's left alone in a parked car. If you have to stop for a meal, for instance, the best thing to do is to leave one family member in charge of your pet; that way, the carrier can be removed from the car and put in the shade, and the cat can benefit from any breeze or air motion. (See Chapter 6 for emergency first aid for heat stroke or stress.)

GOING BY COMMERCIAL CARRIER

It may sometime be necessary for your cat to travel by air; or, if you're going far and your cat's not a good car rider, you may decide that she'd fare better making a quick plane ride to your destination than traveling in a car. Although there's really no way to prepare a cat for air travel, careful planning can make a plane trip less frightening for a cat.

Before making a decision about air travel for your cat, talk it over with the airline, or airlines, that are available. Many won't ship unaccompanied pets at all when the temperatures are either very hot or very cold, and each company has slightly different regulations about allowing pets to ride in the cabin with their owners. All airlines have strict carrier specifications for pets, based on standards set by the Department of Agriculture, whether they're to be shipped or will be accompanied on the trip. If your carrying case doesn't meet your airline's standards, you can usually purchase a suitable reusable plastic container from them. If you're shipping your cat, it's important to book the shortest possible nonstop route, and to be sure that she'll be met the minute she arrives. Most airlines are only too happy to help you to select a direct flight for your cat during nonpeak hours, and many have free pamphlets containing air-travel tips for pets.

If your cat's trip alone will last more than twenty-four hours, attach a water dish and some dry food to the outside of her container, with instructions so that attendants can feed and water her. If for some reason your cat has to stay over between planes in New York's Kennedy Airport, the ASPCA has an Animalport with kennel and veterinary services available. In Los Angeles, Jet Pet in Playa Del Rey provides the same services for pets coming into International Airport. Many other cities have pet-travel services available to meet, care for, or deliver animals to their owners: your airline will probably be able to put you in touch with them, or you can ask your veterinarian for information.

Most interstate buses no longer carry pets at all. Many trains won't allow pets anymore either, and those that do almost always require that they ride in the baggage compartment even if they're accompanied. Since baggage compartments have no temperature controls, it's risky to ship your cat by rail during most seasons. If you're contemplating a train trip with or for your cat, check details with your local ticket seller.

Don't feed your cat for at least four hours before departure time. A healthy cat can go for as long as twenty-four hours without food, and your pet will be much happier traveling if her stomach's not uncomfortably full. Because of the noise level, all cat travelers will benefit from some kind of sedation before they go on a plane or train. The less your pet frets while en route, the sooner she'll be back to normal after her arrival.

Leaving Your Cat Behind When You Go Away

There are a great many circumstances in which it isn't wise or practical to take your cat along with you when you travel or go away on vacation, and there's no reason why you should feel guilty or "mean" about leaving her behind. Actually, most cats prefer not to ride for hours only to be confronted by strange surroundings on arrival. Some cats shouldn't travel at all unless it's absolutely necessary. Very old or very young cats are particularly susceptible to upsets from changes in temperature and surroundings. Sick cats will become sicker when they're moved around; and very high-strung animals not only will be miserable traveling themselves, but will make your life miserable, too.

As long as your cat's physical needs are taken care of, she'll probably be perfectly content to wait patiently for your return. For very short weekend or overnight trips, many owners find that they can safely leave their indoor cat alone. Supplied with plenty of fresh water, dry or semimoist food, and a clean litter tray, a cat can fare quite well alone for as long as two days. If your cat needs company, or if you're going to be away for long, the most satisfactory arrangement for both your cat and you is to arrange for a sitter. If it's impossible to do this for some reason and you decide that you want to board your cat, you should select the place where you'll leave her with a great deal of care.

BOARDING A CAT

Cats' needs are very particular, and most kennels run mainly for dogs aren't equipped to handle cats properly, even if they do accept them. Many years ago when we had Jeffrey we also had a beagle, and one summer when we were going away for two weeks, I arranged to board them both at the same kennel. On our return, the beagle was fine, but Jeffrey was a mess. He was extremely thin and unkempt, and looked glazed and sick. The lady who ran the kennel told me that he had reacted wildly to being kept in a cage next to a lot of strange dogs, had repeatedly bitten the attendants, and wouldn't eat. She wasn't particularly distressed, and said something about cats always doing badly when boarded. It took poor Jeffrey almost a month at home to recover; he wasn't a particularly sensitive or high-strung cat, and I hate to think of what a situation like that would have done to one who was.

If you must board your cat, check the facility very carefully beforehand. Not only should it be clean and free from bad odors, but the attitude of the attendants is important—watch them handling cats to see if they're impatient or caring about their charges. Be sure that your cat will have ample room to move around in; nothing can make a cat more nervous and upset than being closed in a small cage for any length of time. A clean litter tray should be available at all times, and fresh drinking water should be in every cat cubicle. (Sometimes people who run these facilities withhold water in an effort to reduce the volume of urine so that they won't have to change the litter trays so often.) Cats should be entirely isolated from one another by sight and, if possible, they shouldn't be able to hear one another either. The sight, smell, and sound of strange animals will make most cats extremely nervous. Nowadays, there are a number of boarding "hotels" exclusively for cats. They advertise that each cat has a separate room and is given all kinds of individual attention. They are likely to be very expensive. No matter how wonderful a boarding facility sounds, insist on inspecting it carefully before arranging to leave your pet. If you're not allowed to look around, suspect that something's wrong.

It doesn't matter how well a cat boarding kennel is run—there's bound to be a chance that your cat will get sick from airborne viruses. You can help see that your cat is protected from exposure to diseases by making sure that the facility requires a doctor's certificate and up-to-date vaccination record before accepting boarders. Clean cages, well-washed dishes and litter trays, and attendants who are required to wash thoroughly after handling each cat can do a lot to help prevent the spread of infections. The fact remains, however, that nervous stress and emotional upset make all cats very susceptible to infection and disease—that's why a great many veterinarians and cat-care specialists feel that cats should never be boarded.

A SITTER FOR YOUR CAT

By far the best arrangement to make for your cat when you're away is to get a sitter for her. Your cat's sitter can be a friend or family member, a neighborhood youngster who likes animals, or a professional animal-sitter. Since cats can take care of elimination by themselves and don't need to be walked, it's usually not necessary for someone to stay in your house. Most adult cats can get along happily with two daily visits.

An added advantage of this arrangement is that you'll also have a built-in housewatcher, who can take in the mail and papers, turn on some lights, and even water your plants if you wish.

If you're new to a community and don't know anyone to ask to be a cat-sitter, your veterinarian may have a suggestion about where to find one. In many cities professional animal-sitters advertise in the newspaper. Other cat owners may be able to help, or your local school system may have an employment service for students through which you can locate a sitter. An ad in your local newspaper can bring results, too.

If you hire a nonprofessional or a young person to take care of your cat, be sure to work out your financial arrangements ahead of time, and discuss the responsibilities of the job thoroughly. No matter what you decide to pay, it's bound to be a good deal less expensive than today's kennel fees, so you can afford to be generous enough for your sitter to want to do a good job. Even though the actual time the sitter spends taking care of your cat may not add up to many hours of work, the responsibility of regular visits and the thoughtful care you expect your pet to receive should be a consideration when you're deciding on a fee.

If you work out a nonpaying arrangement with a neighbor or family member, don't let the details be too casual. Unless the person who's going to care for your cat knows her feeding and care routines by heart, write everything down, including the phone number of your veterinarian and a friend who knows your cat, if possible. Be sure to leave an ample supply of food and medication if your cat needs it. Show the sitter where your cat carrier is kept, in case she needs to be taken to the doctor, and be sure to alert the sitter about any ongoing medical problems your pet may have. It's particularly nice if your cat-sitter is fond of animals, and

221

will take time out to pay attention to and play with your pet. Over the years, we've been lucky enough to find a series of neighborhood youngsters to sit for our animals who not only enjoy playing with them, but even groom them occasionally.

Before you hire an unknown cat-sitter, it's best to be sure that he or she visits your house to see where things are kept and to meet your pet. If you have any qualms about the sitter's reliability or interest in your pet, don't hesitate to find someone else. Whoever is left in charge of your cat should be aware just how important the job is, and how much you care about your cat's welfare. Some cat owners insist on a "trial run," leaving a new sitter in charge of their pet for a short weekend or overnight before going on a longer trip.

No matter how attentive and loving your cat-sitter has been, if you've been gone for any length of time your cat may decide to punish you for leaving her when you get back. Instead of greeting you happily, she may ignore you completely, refusing to come to you and averting her eyes when you approach her. Don't worry about this—most cats can only manage to keep this act up for a few hours at most, and before you know it, your pet will be purring and demanding attention from you again.

9

Relationships: People and Other Pets

> . . . the cat is selective and . . . the bases
> of his selection are not always clear to the
> human mind.
> —FRANCES AND RICHARD LOCKRIDGE,
> *Cats and People*

Cats may often be devoted to places, but they also crave companionship. They can be just as stubborn about accepting changes in the living creatures around them as they are about adapting to shifts in location.

Anyone who's ever owned a cat can cite examples of her fiercely overt affectionate behavior: they can often also tell stories about conduct obviously triggered by dislike or jealousy.

Cats are usually not particularly subtle about showing how they feel about others. If they like a person or another animal, their affection is clear. Rubbing, purring, and continued efforts to get as close as possible can't be misinterpreted. If they're repeatedly rebuffed by someone they like, cats can become downright annoying in their maneuvers to win recognition. At times, they seem to have a perverse way of recognizing people who are afraid of them, and forcing their attentions on them. A friend of my family's was a true ailurophobe (cat hater; people with this affliction can actually become physically ill when they're near a cat). Every time Mr. Smith came to our house, Pong, who was usually somewhat standoffish with strangers, would immediately walk into the room and jump up on the man's lap, purring loudly and kneading. Mr. Smith would turn slightly pale and hold his hands up at shoulder level so that they didn't accidentally come in contact with Pong, until one of us removed the cat. Pong was quite sensitive and usually knew when he wasn't wanted around, but until we put him outdoors or closed him up somewhere, he wouldn't leave Mr. Smith alone.

Strong aversion on a cat's part is hard to mistake, too. Cats usually demonstrate hatred by attacking or threatening to: hissing, growling, and spitting, an angry cat will circle her enemy on stiff legs with her back arched and the fur on her back and tail standing straight out from her body. Other threatening gestures are a swishing tail, laid-back ears, and flattened whiskers.

Mild dislike is a little harder to recognize. When cats don't especially like a person or another animal, they don't make much of a fuss, they simply disappear. I had a college friend who was severely allergic to cats and used to shoo Pong away every time she saw him. I'm not sure that she didn't also give him a shove or two when no one was looking. Anyway, as soon as she came in the front door, Pong would always vanish and not return until she'd gone.

If a new or disliked person or animal starts to encroach on what a cat considers to be her domain, she may use stronger hints to show how upset she is. What many owners consider to be sudden "bad" behavior by their cat may have been triggered by jealousy.

Although cats are certainly not human, it may help you to understand and deal with your pet's jealous, possessive feelings and reactions if you can think of her in terms of a small child. By realizing how your cat must feel about changes and shifts in your household and its occupants, you may be able to avoid some problems with your pet.

Jealousy

> Jealousy's eyes are green.
> —PERCY BYSSHE SHELLEY,
> *Swellfoot the Tyrant*

It's probably not coincidence that jealousy is often called the green-eyed monster. Cats' eyes are often green, and they can be the most jealous of all animals. A cat's strong territorial feeling usually encompasses people and other pets as well as places. A cat who'll fight to defend her physical property from an intruder will also try to keep the creatures she feels she owns to herself.

Cats who learn to accept newcomers when they're young usually don't feel too threatened by tactfully introduced additions to the household. But cats who've been ''only children'' for a long while and those who've been allowed to become one-person pets can have a difficult time adjusting.

Sometimes there are individual preferences that owners can never figure out. Pickles, for instance, calmly adjusted to the invasion of his house at various times by two puppies and Oliver. But he simply never did like Grace. He never did anything overt about it, but it was obvious that he really didn't like her. I always said that if cats could sneer, Pickles would sneer at Grace every time he saw her.

A tendency to be possessive is usually strengthened as a cat gets older, or if she's not in good health. A cat who's not feeling up to par is apt to be more set in her ways than a healthy, energetic animal. Some cats, too, are just naturally testy and bad-tempered toward anyone they don't know well.

Severe jealousy can bring on a number of different physical and behavioral reactions in a cat. In addition to being emotionally upset by a sudden change in the personnel of the household, some cats become badly frightened, cringing, hiding, and even crying out in terror. Other cats display their resentment by seemingly trying to punish you for their imagined desertion: they'll break training, have sudden bursts of hysterically wild behavior, or suddenly turn destructive, chewing and clawing everything in sight. Stress can trigger physical problems, too—urinary attacks, diarrhea, and an inability to eat. Sometimes stress and fear bring on aggressive behavior and a cat may bite or scratch the intruder, or claw or spray his belongings. There are cats who even turn their frustration and anger on themselves, biting or chewing their own paws or tails until they're raw and bleeding.

If you know your cat pretty well, you may be able to predict how strong her reaction to a newcomer will be. Often, you can do a great deal to offset or allay her feelings of uncertainty and jealousy by thoughtful, tactful handling.

NEW PEOPLE

Cats' noses can be put out of joint by the arrival of a new person in the household, particularly if it's obvious that you're fond of the newcomer. This can be true of adult humans as well as babies.

Adults

If you have a cat who's used to having your undivided attention, the arrival of another person in the house can often upset her. When you know ahead of time that someone is going to be moving into your household, you can help your cat to get used to the idea gradually by allowing her to become familiar with the person's smell. An article of clothing such as a scarf or a sweater can easily accomplish this: leave it lying somewhere that your cat frequents so that she can sniff it often.

Try not to alter your cat's routine suddenly when the newcomer arrives. If you do, she'll associate something unsettling with that person. If you have to change certain rituals, such as the regular time for grooming and play, start to do it before the new person's arrival. If this isn't possible, make the change gradual.

The newcomer can help by participating little by little in your cat's care—grooming, feeding, and playing with her from time to time. Of course, if the new person in your household doesn't particularly like cats, it's a different matter. Your pet will probably sense it immediately and either ignore the person, or go into a persistently annoying attention-getting act. The only solution is for you to act as a moderator, dividing yourself between the two until your cat finally accepts the fact that the newcomer is going to stay.

Babies

Most cats respond to a new baby with some initial interest, followed by boredom when the new creature doesn't play with them. As the baby gets older, a cat will often watch his actions intently, and by the time the infant is old enough to react to a cat, your pet will either display tolerance and patience or will choose to stay a safe distance away most of the time.

You can start to establish a good relationship between your cat and a new baby when you first bring the baby into your home. If your pet is ignored and pushed out of the way during the confusion of the arrival, she's sure to resent it and associate your indifference with the baby. The baby won't know the difference if you stop to pay some attention to your cat the minute you walk in the door—give your pet a special food treat or some catnip. This will make the baby's arrival seem like a positive event to your pet, rather than cause for alarm.

Your cat should be allowed to sniff the baby and explore his room and belongings thoroughly so that she can become accustomed to his scent. If you're at all apprehensive about letting your pet get near the baby, try not to be too obvious about it. Make every effort to relax so that your pet doesn't become alarmed by your tension and think that there's something to be afraid of. The chances of a well-loved pet cat's suddenly striking out at a baby are extremely rare, but, if your pet acts fearful or aggressive and growls or snarls, she should be removed firmly and quickly from the baby's vicinity.

Give your cat a lot of extra attention. While you're ministering to the baby and the cat is in the room, for instance, include her by talking to her the whole time. Keep reminding your pet that you still care for her, and that the baby's going to be her friend. This may seem foolish to you, but even if your cat can't fathom the words you're saying, she'll understand their intent and be reassured by not being shut out of your new activities.

When the baby gets old enough to move around alone, don't allow him to take over any of your cat's belongings. Even the best-natured cat will resent having her toys or dishes grabbed away from her. You may find it's practical to move your pet's food and water dishes off the floor onto a chair or counter until the baby is old enough to be taught not to touch them. Babies can be surprisingly strong, and little fists can really hurt when they pull a cat's fur or tail. Start teaching your baby early not to grab at the cat; usually cats learn quickly to stay at arm's length if they don't want to be yanked at.

The old wives' tale about cats sucking babies' breath simply isn't true, but cats often do like to sleep on people's chests, and a heavy adult cat can make it very difficult for a small baby to breathe. If you're concerned about your cat's getting into the baby's crib when you're not watching and yet want to leave the door open, you can solve the problem by putting a screen across the top of the crib, or over the door opening.

If your cat shows any signs of actively disliking the baby, and your attempts at reassurance don't seem to be working, you'll have to be more careful to separate them. This can be difficult, because if you relegate your formerly well-loved cat to the cellar it will serve only to increase her resentment of the baby. Talk over the problem with your veterinarian. Sometimes a mild tranquilizer will calm an overanxious cat and make her more accepting of the change in her life. If you have a pediatrician who likes animals, he may be able to suggest a remedy. Many doctors, however, have little tolerance for the problems of pets when they conflict with the well-being of their patients and will automatically suggest getting rid of the cat.

Sometimes there's simply no other solution to the problem of a very possessive, jealous cat. This is what happened to Pippin, a four-year old Siamese. Pippin had lived with her mistress since she was a very tiny kitten and was unusually close to her. When her mistress married and moved to a larger house, Pippin surprisingly took it all in stride. But when a new baby came home, Pippin was distraught. She seemed to be terrified of the baby and crept on her belly when she was in the same room. Her mistress tried to make the cat feel secure and loved in every way she could think of, but Pippin only became more and more upset. She also started to become destructive, chewing and ripping everything she could. Nothing seemed to reach Pippin—the veterinarian prescribed tranquilizers, but they only upset her more. After several months, her mistress walked into the baby's room one day and found Pippin sitting on top of a tall dresser peering down at the sleeping baby, snarling and growling. Badly shaken, her mistress took Pippin straight to the veterinarian. He concluded that there was apparently no hope of reconciling Pippin to the baby's presence in the house and that things would probably continue to get worse if they kept the cat.

Because Pippin had been through so much and was obviously not adaptable to change, the owners and the doctor sadly concluded that she could never adjust to the trauma of a new family, so they euthanatized her.

NEW PETS

Cats' reactions to the arrival of a new animal in the household can be just as varied as their responses to new people. A great deal, of course, depends on your pet's basic personality, her relationship to you and other members of the family, and her previous conditioning to other pets. A cat who has had good early experiences with dogs and other cats will usually accept new animals easily as long as her role in the household doesn't change drastically.

Another pet in the house can be beneficial to a cat in several ways. In addition to companionship and entertainment, a new, young pet can help to keep your older cat active, slim, and interested in things. If the household routine is about to change, and your cat is to be left alone more than she has been in the past, another animal can do a great deal to offset her loneliness and sense of desertion. A familiar animal companion can even make a move to a new location less traumatic for a cat.

Again, there are things you can do to help your pet accept a new dog or cat with a minimum of jealousy. In the first place, any new animal you bring into your household when you have an older cat should be young—the younger the better. A mature neutered cat will usually adopt a baby animal. She'll often take over washing, training, and discipline chores. You should allow your older cat almost complete freedom in these matters. She may seem a bit harsh sometimes, but neutered adult cats will almost never really hurt a younger animal. Your pet must be able to establish her right to determine the boundaries for a new youngster—after all, this is her home, and she should be allowed to set the rules. If you continually step in and prevent your cat from disciplining the newcomer, she'll probably become resentful.

If your cat's very possessive of you, it may help if you have someone else bring the new animal into your home. This may seem somewhat extreme, but it can prevent your cat's first waves of jealousy—after all, it isn't your fault if someone else wishes a new animal on you both.

You should be very careful to introduce the new arrival gradually. Cats know who their friends are mainly

231

by smell, so it's a good idea to put a blanket from home belonging to your older pet into the carrier or box in which you intend to bring the new animal home. That way, the new arrival will smell faintly familiar.

No matter how casually your older cat seems to react to the sight and smell of the new animal, it's a good idea not to overdo togetherness at first. Let your cat look at and sniff the newcomer as much as she wants while you're in the room, and then remove the new animal for a while and make a fuss over your older cat. A baby-gate or a playpen is a very good investment if you're getting a new pet (you'll have to line it with wire for a kitten or small puppy). This will allow your older cat to sniff and look all she wants without having to get too close.

Don't allow the newcomer to usurp any thing or place belonging to your older cat. If the baby curls up to sleep in your cat's favorite spot, remove her. Before you know it, your older cat may be inviting the baby to share her food, toys, and sleeping places, but let the initiative come from her.

Cats

Even if you know that you'll eventually want two cats as pets, it's usually not very satisfactory to get two kittens at the same time. In the first place, two kittens who are brought up together will be much more interested in each other than in you. They'll become a unit, and won't need you for companionship and affection. It's harder to train two kittens instead of one—you'll have difficulty knowing who the culprit is when the carpet's soiled or the couch clawed, and the two will often "gang up" to defy you. Everything, in fact, will be more difficult with two young kittens to raise at once. Wild kittens will be wilder, and stubborn kittens will reinforce each other's determination.

The best thing to do if you want more than one cat is to wait until your pet is about a year old before getting a new kitten. By that time you and she will have established a solid relationship. She'll be well settled into household routines, and will know what's expected of her.

Before going out to adopt or buy a new kitten, think about what kind of cat would get along best with your existing pet. You don't want to overwhelm a shy cat with an overly boisterous kitten; on the other hand, if your pet tends to be on the wild side, a calm, relaxed kitten may be very settling for her. Shop just as carefully and thoughtfully for your new kitten as you did for your first, indeed, even more; remember that you have your older cat as well as yourself to please this time.

Follow the suggestions above for avoiding jealousy and let your cat become used to the newcomer gradually. Be especially sure to provide the kitten with her own plates, toys, and bedding; if your older cat is very fastidious, it's even a good idea to have a separate litter tray, at least for a while.

If you're not entirely secure about your cat's reaction to the kitten, don't leave them alone together at first when you're not going to be there. While it's very rare for an older cat intentionally to hurt a kitten, the kitten may badger your older cat so much that she'll lose her temper and strike out. Close the newcomer up and let your older cat have the run of the house; it's safer to keep a new kitten closed up when you're not around, anyway, until you're sure she won't get into trouble. Don't prod or urge your older cat to pay attention to the new kitten. Let the relationship develop in its own time. Your interference may serve only to remind your cat that she should resent the kitten.

Once your cat decides to accept the kitten, she'll probably try to take her over completely. While you should allow your older animal to discipline the kitten in matters concerning her, you can't rely entirely on your pet to teach the kitten everything you want her to learn. Don't let the kitten do anything you don't permit your older pet to do, or you may find that you have to retrain your older cat all over again. She's certainly not going to restrain herself if you allow a newcomer to get away with something.

While your cat is engrossed in getting to know her new playmate, you may be distressed at her seeming uninterest in you. Don't immediately assume that you've made a horrible mistake and have traded one affectionate, companionable cat for two mutually exclusive animals who have no time for you. If you had a good relationship with your cat to begin with, she'll come back to you for attention as soon as the excitement wears off, and soon you'll have two affectionate, companionable cats.

Though it's not common, it's entirely possible that your cat won't accept a newcomer with grace. She may not be particularly overjoyed at having a new kitten in the house, and can react in several ways. She may repeatedly threaten the kitten and hiss at her without actually hurting her. Scolding your cat for acting hostile to the kitten may make her turn to other kinds of bad behavior or self-mutilation that I described before. If she feels no compunction about being overtly hostile, she may take to hitting the baby. In any of these circumstances, you'll have to take drastic measures. If lavish reassurance, praise, and lots of treats don't help, discuss the problem with your veterinarian, who may try tranquilizing your cat slightly for a while. Finally, you may just have to conclude that this particular combination isn't going to work, or that your cat will probably never be able to share your affections with another cat.

Most of our cats have started off their lives in households already populated with other cats and a few dogs, so it's been no surprise that they've usually accepted newcomers with equanimity—each animal retaining his or her territorial rights to certain places and sometimes even certain people. They do have their preferences, however; as I mentioned with Pickles and Grace, they don't always form fast friendships. One thing I've noticed is that it's not a good idea to have three cats at the same time—a trio of cats will often divide into two against one, just as children do. The combinations may vary, but the poor cat who's odd man out can have a pretty miserable time of it for a while. I suppose that the same thing could happen with any odd number of cats, but I've never had more than three at a time.

Dogs

> The gingham dog went, "Bow-wow-
> wow!"
> And the calico cat replied, "Mee-ow!"
> The air was littered, an hour or so,
> With bits of gingham and calico.
>   EUGENE FIELD, "The Duel"

The traditional rivalry between cats and dogs has been greatly exaggerated. The main problem is that many dogs will chase anything that runs, and some thoughtless dog owners encourage their pets to "sic" cats. Left to their own devices, dogs and cats usually coexist very peacefully—they'll often ignore each other completely.

A cat who has been raised with dogs with whom she's had a good experience will usually accept a new puppy into her house very calmly. If the dog is an adult and the cat is grown, the relationship may be strained—a kind of armed truce. There are exceptions. If a cat has been living in a household for long, she can make life pretty miserable for a new adult dog. About six years after we got Peter, the gray long-hair, a friend of the family gave us a two-year-old Boston terrier named Barney. Barney's former owner assured us that he was used to cats, having lived with two of them. As it turned out, the problem was Peter. We hadn't anticipated this, because we knew that Peter had been brought up with a small dog. But Peter apparently took an instant dislike to Barney and decided to show him who was boss. He proceeded to terrorize the dog. He lost no opportunity to badger him: he'd sit on a chair right where he knew Barney would walk, and as soon as Barney started by, Peter would reach out a paw and swipe him across the nose. Peter would also lie on the stairs going to the second floor and when someone called Barney to go for a walk or get his dinner, the cat wouldn't let him go by. He'd hiss and swipe until the poor dog retreated and stood whining for help. Barney was basically good-natured and unaggressive and really didn't know how to cope with Peter's nasty tactics. He'd obviously been brought up to be nice to cats and he couldn't understand Peter's actions. Finally, one day when Peter was again blocking his passage on the stairs and his dinner was waiting in the kitchen, Barney reacted. We heard a commotion in the hall and came out to see Barney holding the big cat down on the floor with his front paws, growling fiercely. When he saw us coming, Barney immediately let Peter go and came over to us sheepishly, expecting to be scolded. Much to his surprise, we applauded him and told him everything was all right. Peter stalked off, head up and tail waving, seemingly unconcerned, but from that day on he never bothered Barney again. They never became friendly, and gave each other a wide berth, but they lived in the same house together calmly until Peter died at age eleven.

In general, dogs pose less of a threat to a cat than another cat in the house does. They can't jump up on things to get at a cat, or sleep in her favorite nest; they don't share a litter tray, or the same food or dishes. Older cats often take over the care of young puppies, just as they do with kittens, making every effort to keep them clean and well-behaved. Again, let the relationship develop naturally if your cat seems motherly. (Altered males, by the way, are often more "motherly" than spayed females.)

If you're adopting a new dog, size should be a consideration. The best-intentioned large dog can be a hazard for a cat, particularly if they're both allowed to run outdoors. A friend's very gentle retriever broke her cat's back when the dog became overexcited and accidentally jumped on the cat. Some small dogs, like terriers and hunting breeds, have a very hard time restraining themselves from chasing anything that moves, and can also accidentally injure a cat in their exuberance.

Follow the advice I gave about selecting a new kitten when you choose a puppy to live with your cat. Try to get a dog whose temperament will complement your cat's. Again, introduce them gradually, closing the puppy up the minute you think that your cat has had enough. An added precaution in case your cat gets carried away is to trim her nails well before letting her play with the puppy.

It's a good idea to bear in mind that if your cat has always lived with dogs, she may sometimes need to be reminded that it's not smart to trust every dog she comes upon outdoors.

Our dogs and cats have often become really close. I've told you about how Wilbur always takes a walk with our dogs, and if one of the dogs has been away for a while, Wilbur always greets him fondly on his return with a nose-touch and a purr. Pickles and a small poodle we had used to curl up and sleep together all the time, and when the dog was killed by a car, Pickles spent several days looking and calling for him.

VISITING PETS

The best way to deal with visiting pets is to make it clear that they're not welcome. This may be difficult if your friends or relatives have a "love me, love my pet" attitude, but if you stick to your guns, they may respect your wishes.

It's asking the impossible to expect your cat to accept a strange adult animal visitor into her territory with equanimity. One of two reactions, or a combination of both, is likely: she'll disappear completely, sometimes not even appearing for meals; or she'll stand her ground and defend her territory. Either way, everybody will be miserable.

When you know ahead of time that company is coming with a pet, offer to make a reservation at a local boarding facility. If this doesn't work, and you can't avoid an animal visitor, there are several things that you can do to make the whole thing less traumatic. Avoid confrontation at all costs. The visitor, not your pet, should be confined. You can make him comfortable in one room (usually the bedroom his owners will occupy is best), and insist that he be taken out only when your cat is safely closed up somewhere else.

Never allow a visiting animal to use your pet's things—provide him with his own dishes, toys, and bedding.

No matter how careful you are to separate your cat from the visitor, she's still bound to be upset by the stranger's presence in the house, and will need a lot of extra attention and reassurance from you.

Loneliness: Grieving

> Far in the stillness a cat
> Languishes loudly.
> WILLIAM ERNEST HENLEY,
> "In Hospital. Vigil"

Because they're often very strongly attached to people and other animals, cats can become very lonely when they're suddenly deprived of a lot of attention and affection. Severe, prolonged loneliness can lead to depression, and a depressed cat will often stop eating and taking care of herself. Some cats even turn to self-mutilation when they're extremely lonely and bored: this happens most often with lost or abandoned cats who suddenly find themselves impersonally tossed into a cage at a pound or shelter.

A lonely, bored pet cat won't usually turn to such extreme actions, but she may take to other kinds of unusual or "bad" behavior in the house. As I said before, getting her a companion may help. If you or your cat don't particularly want another animal, you could arrange for an interested person to come in several times a day to spend time with your cat.

The sudden loss of a well-loved animal or human companion can lead a cat to grieve. Pong, the Siamese, first came to live with us along with Ping, his sister. The two kittens were inseparable, playing and rolling together all day long and sleeping twined up in a ball. When we first had them, we kept them closed up in a large room on the top floor of the house when we weren't home; later on, they slept there. One day, when they were about three months old, the kittens were running around and playing quite wildly on the top floor landing. Ping somehow fell through the banister. When she landed three floors below, her neck was broken and she was dead. We were all very upset, but Pong was devastated. He continually searched the entire house, calling loudly, and wouldn't settle down to sleep or allow himself to be petted or stroked. He refused to eat at all, and finally after a couple of days, we decided to force-feed him. After about a week, Pong settled down a bit and started to demand a great deal of attention from us. He'd apparently come to terms with the fact that Ping wasn't coming back, and we were the only substitutes he could find. From that time on, Pong was a particularly demanding cat.

Sudden, unexpected family emergencies can upset everyone. Sometimes it's hard to remember that a cat may be suffering from upset, too, and can be feeling lonely and neglected. If your cat's a well-loved companion, she'll usually be sensitive to the moods of the people around her and may be fearful. An extra pat or special treat can help your cat to know that you haven't forgotten her, even during a period of family turmoil.

Cats have no sense of time, so even the temporary absence of a favorite person or other pet can sometimes cause a cat to grieve. If she's very dependent on that individual, she may refuse to eat or allow anyone else to care for her. Be gentle and understanding with a pet who's sad and lonely and seems to be missing someone—your kind gestures will usually make her feel better and may establish a new bond between you and your cat.

What to Do If You Can't Keep Your Cat

> Hang sorrow! care'll kill a cat.
> BEN JONSON,
> *Every Man in His Humour*

Needless to say, when you take it upon yourself to adopt or buy a kitten or cat, you should assume that you're going to care for her for her entire natural life span. But situations come up which you can't possibly predict, and you may have to make the difficult decision that you can't keep your pet anymore.

When Pippin's mistress, for instance, brought home the tiny Siamese kitten, she assumed that they'd be together for many years; later, the welfare of her baby changed her plans. Less drastic problems, such as severe allergies that suddenly develop, can cause you to find you can't keep a cat. You may have to move somewhere where pets aren't welcome. These are just a few of the possible reasons why your cat may not be able to live with you anymore.

Your problem isn't very serious if the new kitten you brought home just isn't working out. Although you can become very fond of a kitten in an amazingly short time, a relatively new young cat won't have the same kind of relationship with you as an older cat will, and neither of you should be too devastated by separation. If the kitten was purchased from a breeder, she can often be returned to her original owner. If not, well-brought-up kittens are quite easy to place in a new home.

An older cat is another matter. Not only is it a lot harder on you to give up a good friend and companion, but it's often very difficult for an older cat to adjust to

241

an entirely new place on top of learning how to depend on a whole new set of people.

The best solution, no matter what your cat's age, is to find someone who already knows and cares for your pet and would like to have her. The transition will be somewhat easier for the animal because the person won't be entirely unknown to her. If there's time, you can ease your cat's adjustment by arranging to have her new owner spend some time alone with her in your home.

If you don't know anyone who'd like your cat, talk to your veterinarian. He may know someone who would like to have a pet who's already acclimatized to a household. Again, you can help smooth over the transition by letting the prospective owner get to know your pet in your house before taking her away.

Of course, you'll be sure to pack up all of your cat's belongings, particularly bedding or a favorite sweater or blanket. Familiar objects and smells will help to make her adjustment easier. If your pet has certain routines that she enjoys, or particular food preferences, write them down, along with a record of her immunizations. If the new owner is friendly and won't mind, you may want to make arrangements to visit your pet once in a while. If, however, your cat is very attached to you, this may not be a good idea—her acceptance of her new owners will probably go faster if she's not constantly reminded of you.

If there's a pet relocation agency in your area, your veterinarian will probably know about it; if not, look in the Yellow Pages. These nonprofit agencies are devoted to the welfare of unwanted pets, and the people who run them are very careful about placing animals in suitable homes. They usually charge a fee to both the past and the future owners—the money is used to cover the cost of advertising and medical care of the adoptees (most won't handle unneutered cats, for instance, and will arrange to have them altered or spayed). After meeting you and your cat, the agency generally places a group advertisement in a local paper, including your pet and others. They then interview and screen all applicants for pets and when they think they've found a suitable home for your particular cat, they'll arrange for a meeting in your home. If the applicant decides to adopt your pet, and you're optimistic about the chances for success, the placement will be tried on a temporary basis. If it doesn't work, your cat will usually be returned to you by the agency, which will continue to try to place her. In rare cases, the agency will keep your cat until she can be replaced. The advantages of using a service like this to place your cat are twofold: you don't have to handle and screen a lot of calls, but can leave it to experienced people; in addition, once the service accepts your fee, they're committed to work until they find a suitable home for your cat. These placement agencies are often in direct conflict with local humane societies or shelters, so don't ask your dogcatcher about them.

The worst possible thing that you can do to a cat who needs a home is to take her to a pound or animal shelter. They perform a needed service when it comes to dogs, but they just aren't equipped to handle cats properly. There are health hazards that can't be avoided because of overcrowding, and even a very young kitten can be badly upset by being put in a cage with a number of unknown cats. The psychological stress for an older cat who's used to living in a caring home can't be overstated. A healthy, resilient kitten who is adopted quickly will eventually recover from her bad experience, and the younger the cat the more quickly she'll bounce back (Wilbur, for instance, turned out just fine). If a less adaptable cat spends more than a few days in a pound or shelter, however, her nerves and temperament are apt to suffer permanent damage. Most shelters or pounds won't even consider taking a cat over a certain age (three or four years) for adoption—they know how badly she'll react to being there, and they realize that it's often impossible to place an older cat in a new home.

If you can't find a suitable home for your older cat yourself, it's immeasurably better to end her life kindly than to subject her to the certain terror of the pound. If you've had a good relationship with your cat and she's been well cared for all of her life, you shouldn't agonize too much over the decision to have her put to sleep. Try to think in her terms and not to anthropomorphize—you mustn't let your emotions and guilt feelings interfere with making a move that will ensure that your cat won't have to live the rest of her life in an agony of fear and confusion. Because she'll have no way of knowing what's going to happen, your cat won't be afraid. All she'll be aware of is a quiet, peaceful sleep. Most veterinarians will permit owners who request it to stay by their pet's side during the process, so your cat's last memory will be of you stroking her (see p. 253 for more details on euthanasia).

10

The Older Cat

Life will go on forever,
With all that a cat can wish;
Warmth, and the glad procession
Of fish and milk and fish.
—ALEXANDER GRAY, "On a Cat Ageing"

Cats grow old very gracefully, and many of them stay active and alert until the day they die. Inherited tendencies, diet, and general care will all contribute to determining just when your pet starts to show her age. While the average life expectancy of a well-cared-for cat is about twelve or thirteen years, many cats live well for twenty years or more.

It's often hard for owners to realize that their cat is getting elderly. The signs are usually gradual and very subtle. The first thing you may notice is that your pet sleeps more than she used to. She'll crave warmth, and will always choose sun, heat, or a warm body to sleep near. If she's an indoor-outdoor cat, she may not go out as much, and will probably stick close to home when she does. She may not initiate play with you or other pets very often, and when she does play, she'll tend to tire or lose interest quite fast. On the other hand, she'll almost certainly be much more demanding of affection and attention from favorite people than she formerly was; you'll find that she'll continually try to get as close to you as possible, and will seem to crave frequent reassurance and petting.

Keeping an Older Cat Happy and Well

The need for constant reminders of your consistent love and care is probably related to most older cats' dislike of change in their usual routines. Old cats are not very adaptable, and any alteration in the people or things around them can upset them. You can avoid this kind of stress by introducing any necessary changes gradually.

If you have to go away, don't leave an old cat alone, even for a day; and don't board her unless she's very familiar with the place. Arrange for your senior citizen to be cared for at home by a loving person.

Your pet will usually see to it that she's warm enough, but you must be sure that she doesn't get chilled accidentally—older cats are particularly susceptible to respiratory infections. As a cat ages, her metabolism is less able to regulate body temperatures, so it's essential to keep her from becoming too cold (or too hot, by the way). Provide a cozy sleeping place with high sides to keep her out of drafts, and be very careful not to forget and let her stay out all night, especially if it's cool or wet.

Some older cats don't need to be reminded to keep moving, but others are more sedentary. If your senior citizen tends to sit around a lot, encourage her to stay active. Another pet may help to get her going, but don't wait for your cat to decide to play—tempt her to chase a piece of string or fetch a light ball. Try to make her move around some every day. It will stimulate her circulation, keep her joints flexible, perk up

246

her appetite and digestion, and keep her alert and interested in what's going on around her.

All cats like to be clean, but as your cat gets old, she may not be able to keep herself as neat as she used to. A little extra grooming care from you will be greatly appreciated. An absolutely clean litter tray is a necessity for an older cat—otherwise her increased sensitivity may prevent her from using it.

If your cat seems to become clumsy and slow as she ages, be very patient with her. She'll be confused and upset at her sudden lack of grace and style, and if you laugh at her you'll only depress her more. Pretend that you don't notice her uncharacteristic actions, and give her a pat to show that you still think she's fine. If she has urinary or digestive problems that cause her to break training, don't scold—again, she'll be just as distressed as you are. See to it that she gets medical help as fast as possible.

By providing a calm, secure environment for your older cat and treating her with considerate, loving care, you'll not only make her last years pleasant and happy, but you may even be able to ensure that she'll live longer, thanks to the absence of stress and tension.

DIET

An older cat's reduced activity level coupled with changes in her metabolism will usually mean that she'll need fewer calories in order to maintain her health and current body weight. You can cut back on the number of calories your cat gets each day without making her feel hungry if you eliminate some of the fat in her diet. If you've been adding extra fat, cut the amount in half. If the food you've been feeding your pet already has a high fat content, substitute a food with less fat for part of her daily feeding.

It's important not to allow your older cat to get too fat. Once an older cat's put on a lot of excess weight, it's very difficult for her to lose it, and overweight is particularly damaging to an aging cat's health and well-being.

Smaller portions of food served at more frequent intervals not only will keep your cat from thinking you're starving her, but will be easier for her digestive system to handle as she ages. If your pet has lost some teeth, she may not be able to chew as well as she used to, so pay attention to the size of the pieces of food you give her, and soften dry food slightly if she can't handle it.

If your cat doesn't seem to be utilizing her food well and starts to become too thin, your veterinarian may decide to add some easily absorbed supplements to her diet. Consult him about any feeding questions you have concerning your older cat.

There are particular feline medical conditions that require specialized diets. Fortunately, nowadays these special diets are readily available through your veterinarian. If your cat has a heart, liver, or kidney ailment, or is extremely obese, your veterinarian will be able to provide you with a diet especially made to meet her specific problem.

ROUTINE HEALTH CARE

It's especially important for an older cat to have frequent checkups. She should visit the doctor at least once a year; every six months is even better, particularly if she's very old or has any specific medical problems.

At this stage in her life, a doctor who knows your pet well will be able to spot any significant changes you might miss. What's more, it will help both you and your pet to have a well-established relationship with a doctor you both trust in case anything should go wrong.

Most veterinarians are very aware of how badly older cats react to the stress of a hospital stay, and will do everything they can to avoid the necessity of keeping your cat for any length of time. This is another excellent reason for regular office checkups: when a condition is diagnosed early it can generally be taken care of at home.

Physical Problems of an Older Cat

Between veterinary visits, watch your older cat carefully for signs of physical problems. Don't let anything that concerns you go for long—just like very young kittens, old cats can sicken fast.

If your formerly good-natured cat suddenly becomes testy, you can be pretty sure that something's hurting her. Don't just assume that she's simply getting cranky in her old age. Have her looked over thoroughly for the cause.

If your cat starts to break training and urinates outside her pan, something's undoubtedly wrong. Although older cats' capacity to hold urine can diminish and cause them occasionally to make mistakes, greatly increased water drinking, which leads to a constantly full bladder and frequent accidents, is usually a sign of kidney or bladder trouble. Your veterinarian should be consulted right away.

Sometimes older cats have a problem with dribbling urine owing to a loss of muscle control. If your cat's troubled by this, she'll usually try to keep herself clean when she's awake. It may be a problem when she's sleeping—if so, put rubber or plastic sheeting under her bedding.

An older cat whose digestive system is chronically upset shouldn't be ignored. Although all cats may occasionally get diarrhea, constipation, or an upset stomach, these conditions can weaken an aging cat if they go on for long. Vomiting, sudden weight loss or gain, excessive appetite or thirst, can all be signs of a number of conditions that require immediate attention by a veterinarian.

SOME OTHER COMMON AILMENTS OF OLDER CATS

Don't be alarmed if you think that your cat's suffering from one of these ailments. Most are not life-threatening in themselves, and respond to early treatment.

Arthritis

If you notice that your cat seems lame when she first gets up from sleeping, she's probably developed some arthritis in her joints. This is a condition that has developed over a period of time, and there's really nothing that you or a doctor can do to cure it now. Most cats don't seem to be troubled by stiffness once they're up and moving around, and there's no need to medicate them. Unfortunately, many painkillers that work for people and other animals are toxic for cats, so unless your pet is in severe pain, most doctors prefer not to give anything for arthritis.

If a cat is overweight, slimming her down will put less strain on aching joints.

Ears

If your cat seems to ignore you when you call her, she may have a slight hearing loss. If you want to test her, clap your hands sharply behind her head. It's common for cats to suffer from gradual deafness, and there's nothing that can be done to prevent or cure it.

Eyes

A common older-cat eye condition that often alarms owners is a whitish film or haze over their pet's eyes. This slight film is a natural outgrowth of aging and doesn't affect a cat's vision.

Cataracts, which appear as very white spots on the lens of the eye, are not commonly found in cats. They do, of course, affect vision. While cataracts can be removed surgically, most veterinarians advise against nonessential surgery for any older animal.

Sometimes cats become susceptible to conjunctivitis as they age. If your cat's eyes are running and red, suspect that this may be the cause and have your veterinarian take a look. Medicinal ointment will usually clear it up.

Growths

Tumors can appear on a cat at any time, but age seems to increase the chances of a cat's developing a growth. Some, of course, are internal and impossible for you to detect. You should check your older cat regularly for external growths, however. Areas where they're particularly likely to appear are in a cat's mouth, and on the mammary glands of females. They can often be easily removed and should always be seen by a veterinarian.

Heart Trouble

Although heart trouble often seems to appear suddenly in a cat, it's always been developing for a long time. Overweight and a lifetime of a too-rich diet can be contributing factors, but so can simple aging.

If your cat suddenly has trouble breathing, with a rapid pulse, and refuses to move or eat, get her to the veterinarian immediately. There are drugs that can be given to help a cat with heart trouble. Your doctor will also undoubtedly put your cat on a special low-salt diet.

Mouth and Teeth

It's especially important to keep your older cat's mouth and teeth in good condition. She should have regular mouth examinations, and her teeth ought to be cleaned to retain their health. If she seems to have any difficulty chewing, suspect a loose or infected tooth. Extractions of diseased teeth are sometimes necessary, and will relieve your cat's discomfort. Most cats can chew perfectly well without a full complement of teeth.

Caring for an Invalided Older Cat

As I said before, your veterinarian will probably suggest that your sick older cat will fare better in familiar surroundings than in a hospital. Taking care of an older cat who's not well requires essentially the same routine as caring for a younger animal (see "Caring for a Sick Cat at Home" in Chapter 5).

The important difference is that your older pet will need just about twice as much love and reassurance as a younger cat does. If your household can accommodate it, it may work out better if you can locate your older cat's sickroom in a fairly central spot instead of closing her up in a quiet room away from everything. A large lined carton or box placed in the kitchen or living room where the family gathers may help your old pet to feel less deserted and lonely. The whole box can then be moved to be near you at night. You probably don't have to worry about disturbing your cat unless your household is very noisy—old cats can usually sleep through a lot of noise as long as it's familiar household activity.

At this point, you don't need to worry about spoiling your pet, so you can give her lots of special food treats if she's allowed to have them, and an overdose of love.

If your cat doesn't seem to be getting better and starts to fail, consult with your doctor. He'll probably advise you to continue to keep her calm, warm, and comfortable. If she's not in any pain or distress, keep her with you even if she becomes very weak and isn't eating. She needs your support and care, and you and your family will feel better if you can continue to keep her comfortable in familiar surroundings until the end.

Euthanasia: A Difficult Decision

If, on the other hand, your cat is obviously in pain or distress, you may feel that it's kinder to have her "put to sleep." Don't rush into this decision. Talk it over with your veterinarian. By now he knows you and your pet well, and can help you make an intelligent choice. If you react too emotionally and impulsively in your concern over your cat's pain, you may regret it later on. Avoid listening to well-meaning friends and family members who urge you to put your pet "out of her misery," and rely instead on the doctor and your own good judgment to help you decide what to do, based on medical facts. If your cat can be cured or allowed to live a pain-free year or more longer, you may want to keep her alive.

You may conclude, however, that it would be cruel to try to keep your cat alive. Based on your doctor's advice, it may seem better for your pet to allow her release. Another valid deciding factor can be cost. If it's going to be very expensive to keep your cat alive and pain-free, practical considerations may force you to conclude that you simply can't afford it.

Once you've made a well-thought-out decision to euthanatize your cat, you should proceed as quickly as possible. As I said in the previous chapter, you don't have to worry that your pet will be afraid. Cats can't know or anticipate what's going to happen; therefore they can't fear it.

The process is quick and painless. The doctor injects an overdose of an anesthetic into a vein in the cat's leg. The cat simply slips off into permanent unconsciousness in a matter of seconds without any pain or apprehension.

If you feel that you want to be present, ask your doctor and he'll probably allow it. But don't feel bad if you can't bear to be there. Say good-bye to your cat ahead of time, and rest assured that the doctor and his helpers will be kind and loving to her.

Afterward: Coping with the Death of a Well-Loved Cat

> Pet was never mourned as you,
> Purrer of the spotless hue.
> —THOMAS HARDY,
> "Last Words to a Dumb Friend"

Whether your cat dies of natural causes or is euthanatized, you and your family will have to come to terms with her death. Just as doctors are gradually becoming aware of the benefits for many people of owning a pet, so there's more attention being paid to the emotional impact of a beloved pet's death. Recently, a great deal of work has been done on the psychology of pet loss and its effects on people. More and more, professionals who deal with both animals and humans are realizing that it's not "silly" for a perfectly rational person, adult or child, to be truly upset at the loss of an animal companion.

If a pet's death is sudden or unexpected it can be a real shock to her owners, and may lead to severe guilt feelings. Children especially can be worried and frightened by a pet's death, particularly if it's unexplained. It's important to keep them informed if a cat is unwell or very old—and if a child is old enough, he should be included in decisions about the pet, even a decision to euthanatize.

BURIAL OR CREMATION

A child should never be discouraged from grieving openly for a dead cat, and if he's very upset it may help if you can show him where the pet is. Adults, too, sometimes feel better if a beloved pet's body or ashes are buried in a place they can visit.

If you live in the country or have a large suburban yard, it may be possible for your pet to be buried on your property (in most places now it's against the law; your veterinarian will probably know the local restrictions). First, of course, you'll have to have the body embalmed and put into a sealed coffin.

If it isn't possible to bury your pet's body, you can arrange to have her cremated and keep or bury the ashes if you want. There are pet cemeteries in almost every part of the country, and you can buy a marker in a wide range of costs for your pet if you wish.

When your pet dies in the doctor's office, making these arrangements usually isn't difficult. If she dies at home, you'll have to wrap her body and take it to the nearest animal hospital.

Most animal shelters and pounds will take care of your cat's body for a small fee. If you don't care about preserving her remains, this is probably the easiest and least expensive solution.

THE NICEST TRIBUTE

The nicest tribute that you can give a well-loved cat who has just died is to adopt a new kitten right away. Don't think of the new pet as in any way "taking the place" of her predecessor. This is not the point, and will only lead to unfortunate comparisons. The point is—now that your former cat has taught you just how delightful living with a cat can be, you can't imagine not always having a feline pet to share your life.

As an experienced cat owner, you should have no trouble choosing and raising a new kitten, and before you know it, you and she will be "best friends."

APPENDIX

A Selected Reading List

There are a lot of cat books around. Some of them have achieved the status of modern classics: *Cat Catalog*, edited by Judy Fireman, is billed as "The Ultimate Cat Book"—and it certainly is a grand pastiche of information that's both useful and irrelevant for a cat owner. If you haven't seen it, you should. B. Kliban's cat cartoons, which appear in books, on calendars, notepaper, and so forth, are not only amusing but are extremely incisive commentaries on the essence of cats. If you've never really looked at them, do. Most of the pamphlets and booklets offered as premiums by cat-food manufacturers contain sound, if limited, information. They're usually well worth sending for.

I've found no really helpful books about breeds of cats. Most are attractive, and contain information about feline genetics, color variations, and Point Standards for showing cats, but nothing about the personality and temperament of each breed. These books are usually very expensive, so I suggest that if you want to see what the various breeds look like, peruse them in your local library.

Of the many cat books I've read, these seem to me to be the best in their categories.

Natural History and Behavioral Studies
Muriel Beadle, *The Cat* (A Fireside Book, Simon & Schuster, 1979). This is a fascinating, well-written book about the history, biology,

257

and behavior of cats. As the author states in her introduction, she set out to find the answers to "questions of the sort that have occurred to me from time to time in connection with my own cats." From chapters called "The Chase" through "How Sociable?" to "Man and Beast Together" she leads you to a better understanding of just what makes your own cat tick.

In *Understanding Your Cat* (Coward, McCann & Geoghegan, 1974; Bantam Books, 1977), Dr. Michael W. Fox explores some of the same ground, but with more practical applications for the cat owner. Although this book can be rather hard to use as a resource because of its lack of chapter divisions, it's very interesting reading for cat owners.

Health Care
The Well Cat Book, by Terri McGinnis, D.V.M. (Random House, 1975), is probably the best book of its kind I've ever seen. It covers all aspects of feline health care thoroughly. In the Diagnostic Medicine section, there's even a separate Index of Signs, designed for quick and efficient use when your pet is ailing. Clear illustrations by Tom Reed, D.V.M., well-thought-out headings, and numerous marginal notes make this a book that is very easy to use. A "must" for all cat owners.

The Complete Kitten & Cat Book, by Norman H. Johnson, D.V.M., and Saul Galin (Harper & Row, 1979), is indeed "complete"—so much so, in fact, that it can be confusing to the average reader. Because it covers so much material—from breeds, to wild cats, to nutrition and health care—you often have four widely-spaced page references for something as simple as flea collars. The information in this book seems sound; it's the organization that makes the book unnecessarily difficult and cumbersome to use.

Cookbooks
The Healthy Cat & Dog Cook Book, by Joan Harper (Soodik Printing Co., 1975), is based on the premise that it's possible to feed pets economically and nutritionally by cooking for them yourself, using "natural" recipes. Some of the recipes seem difficult and time-consuming to me, and the emphasis is on dogs, but this little book is nice to have in case the urge to cook for your cat comes over you.

Dr. Terri McGinnis' Dog & Cat Good Food Book (Taylor and Ng, 1977), illustrated by Margaret Choi, is more than a cookbook. It contains a lot of good nutritional and feeding information interspersed with recipes and suggestions for preparing a good diet for cats from homemade foods. Full of charts, tables, and illustrations, this is an attractive as well as useful book for cat owners.

Just for Entertainment

All My Patients Are Under the Bed: Memoirs of a Cat Doctor, by Dr. Louis J. Camuti, with Marilyn and Haskel Frankel (Simon & Schuster, 1980). An eighty-seven-year-old veterinarian who still makes house calls (although he now insists that patients who live above the second floor in walk-up buildings be brought downstairs to be examined in the hallway), reminisces about his many years as "the Albert Schweitzer of the cat world." A delightful and sometimes very funny book.

Do Cats Think? by Paul Corey (Jove/HBJ, 1978) is a delightful book about the author's relationship with a number of cats over the years. You may not agree with all of his ideas and conclusions about cats, but the stories are lively and interesting. The book is written with warmth and humor and, despite its rather silly title, is well worth reading if you like cats.

Eric Gurney's *How to Live with a Calculating Cat* (Pocket Books, 1976) continues to be a very funny book. The nine-page cartoon on pilling a cat still makes me laugh every time I see it!

The Fur Person, by May Sarton (W. W. Norton, 1970) is the story of how Tom Jones, a Gentleman Cat, sets out to seek a suitable housekeeper to settle down with. His adventures during the search and with the two housekeepers he adopts are amusingly told. Although it seems somewhat affected at times, this book is nevertheless generally charming. I especially liked "The Ten Commandments of a Gentleman Cat."

Doreen Tovey's *Cats in the Belfry* (Robin Clark, Ltd., 1978) and *A Comfort of Cats* (St. Martin's Press, 1979) will especially delight Siamese lovers. These books (the only two of the number of books Mrs. Tovey's written which I've read) consist of tales of the author's and her husband's life with some very strong-willed Siamese cats in a formerly idyllic English country setting. There's always at least one blue-point female and one seal-point male to make life in the Tovey cottage fraught with "interesting" incidents. These are very funny books.

A Celebration of Cats, edited by Jean Burden (Popular Library, 1976), contains hundreds of poems about cats: Angelic, Demonic, Mysterious, Antic, Wild, and "Undefined." Cat lovers will enjoy owning this book.

259

Appendix

T. S. Eliot's *Old Possum's Book of Practical Cats* (Harcourt, Brace & World, 1967) continues to be about the most delightful collection of humorous cat poems that exists. Written as gifts for friends who were cat owners, these fourteen poems are still bound to please any cat lover.

INDEX

Index

Index

Index

About the Author

Elizabeth Randolph is the Pet Care editor for "Family Circle" magazine. She is also the author of Fawcett's HOW TO HELP YOUR PUPPY GROW UP TO BE A WONDERFUL DOG, and THE BASIC BIRD BOOK. Ms. Randolph lives with her family in Mamaroneck, New York.

Finally Fawcett has the purrr-fect Pet Care Books